Latina Girls

HOT SEXY LATINA LINGERIE GIRLS MODELS PICTURES

By **EROTICA PHOTO ART LOVER**

Copyright © Latina Girls

ALL RIGHTS RESERVED. NO PART OF THIS DOCUMENT MAY BE REPRODUCED OR TRANSMITTED IN ANY FORM OR BY ANY MEANS, ELECTRONIC, MECHANICAL, PHOTOCOPYING, RECORDING, OR OTHERWISE, WITHOUT PRIOR WRITTEN PERMISSION OF EROTICA PHOTO ART LOVER.

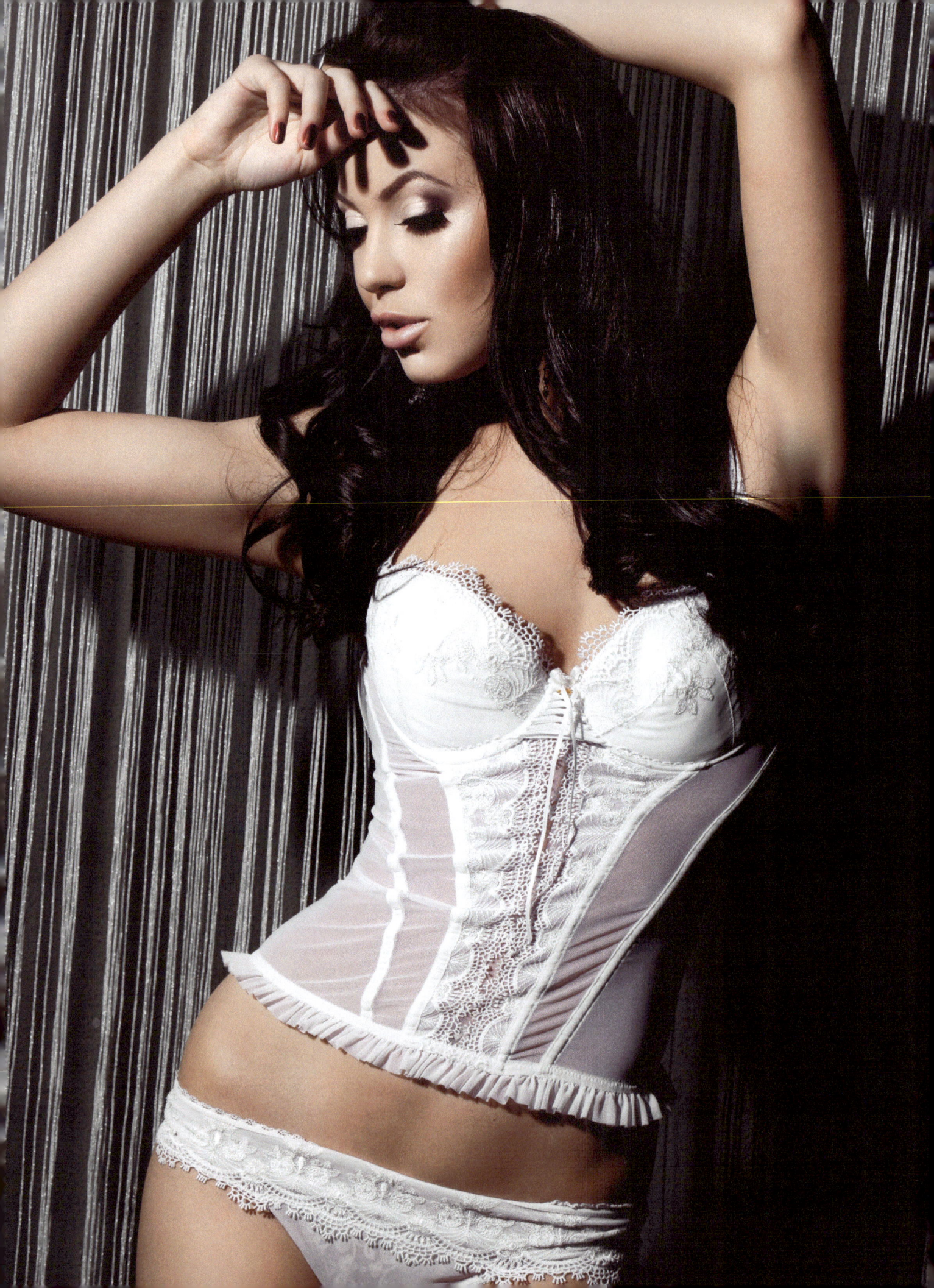

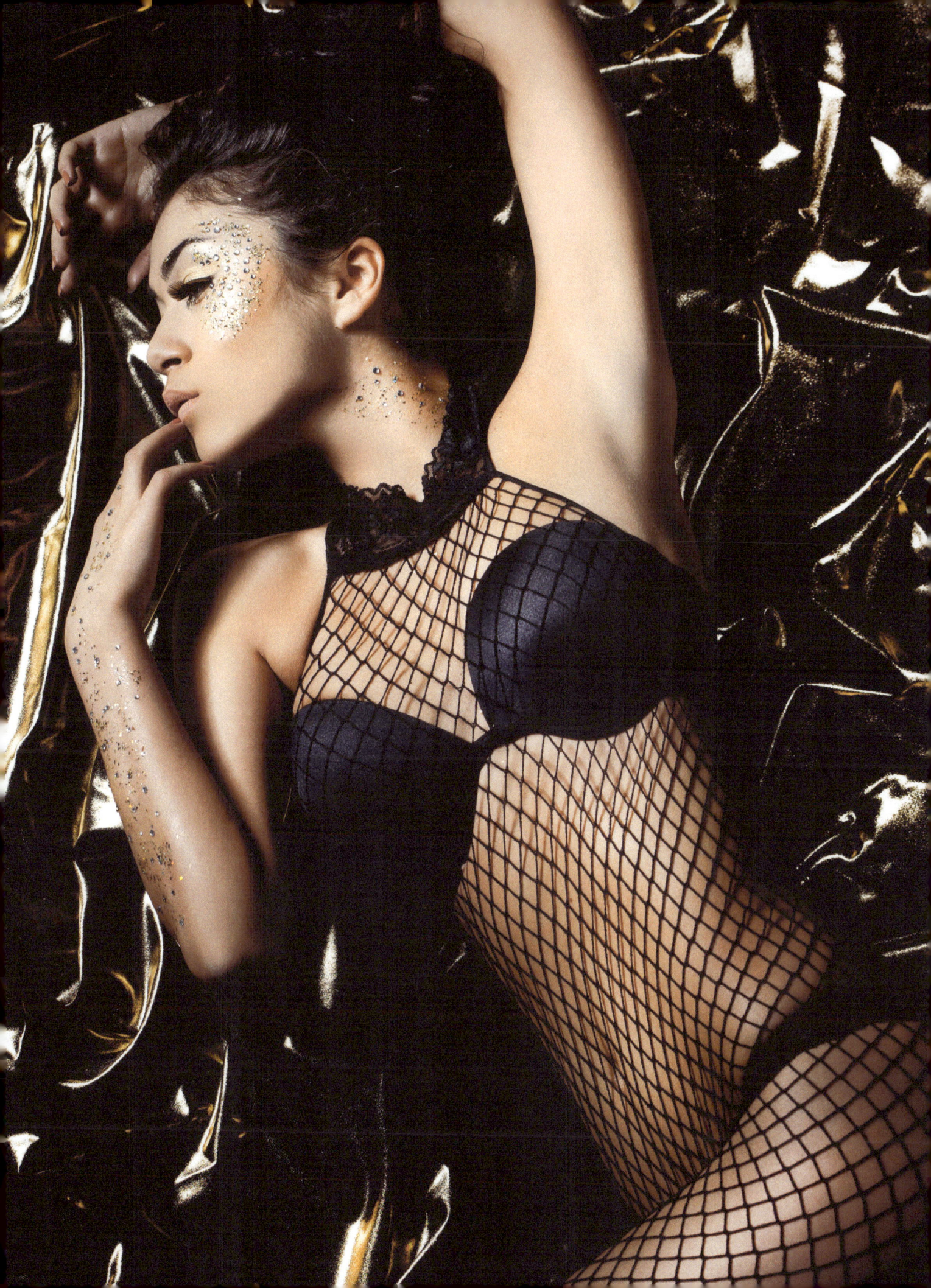

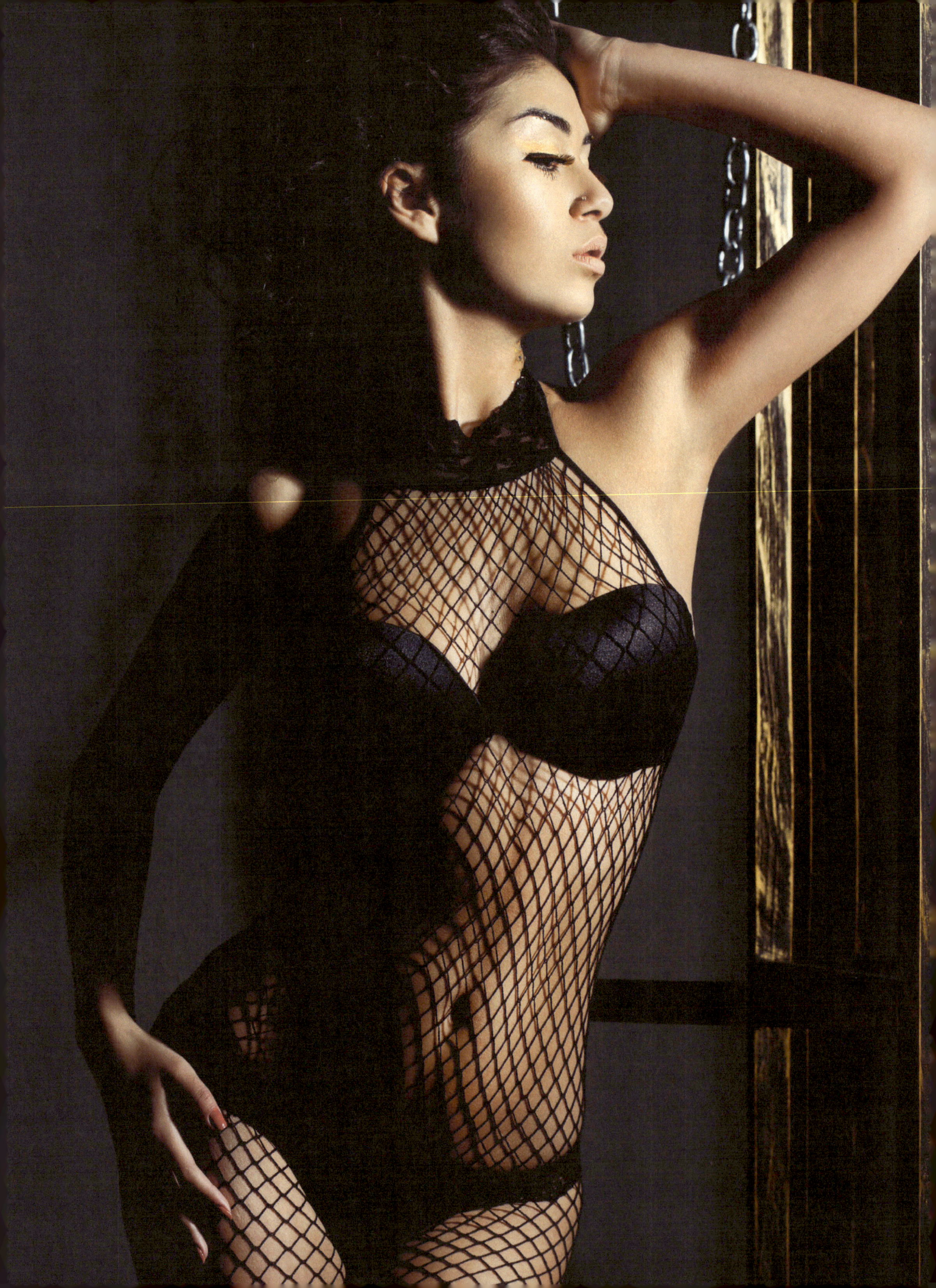

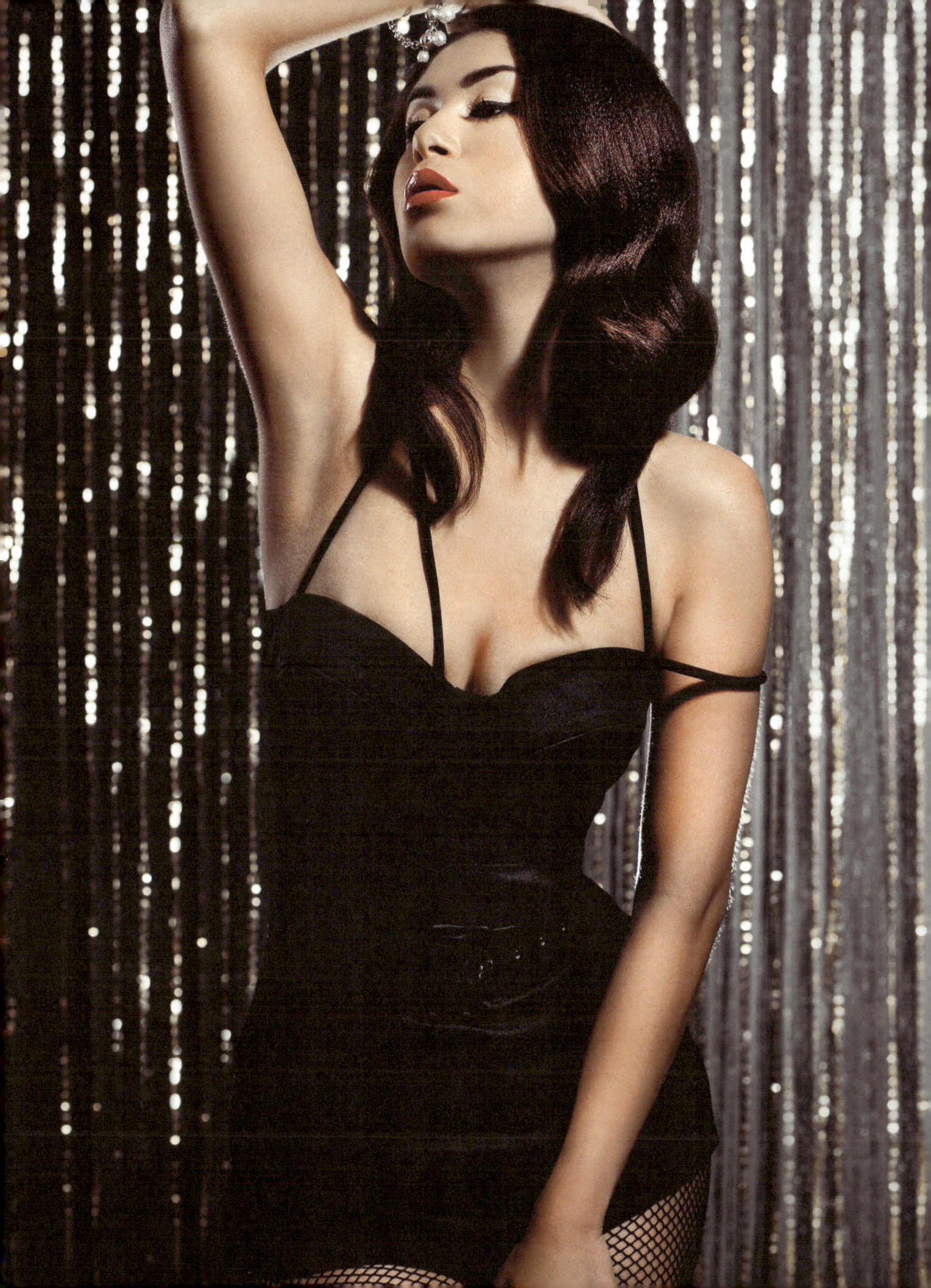

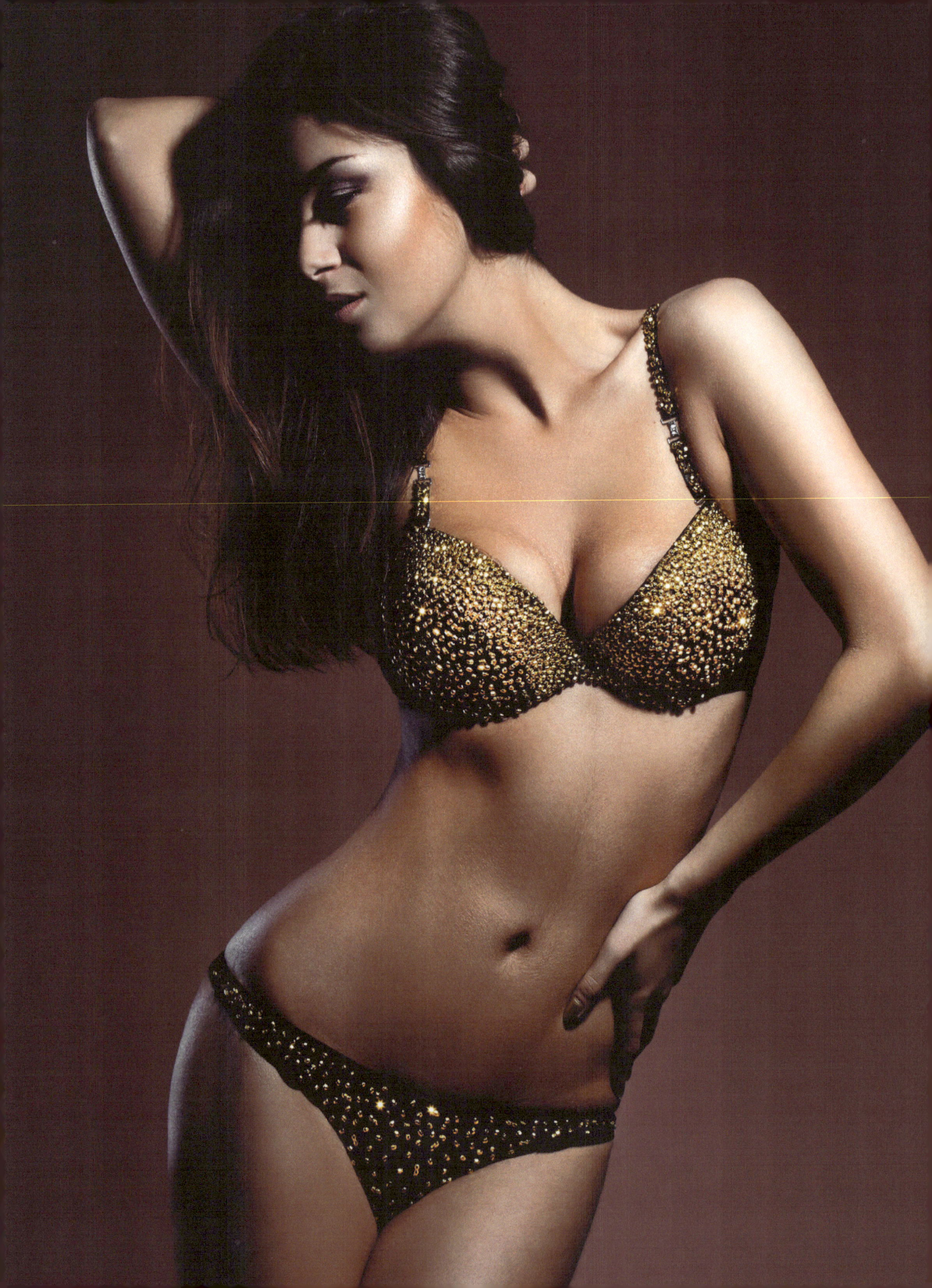

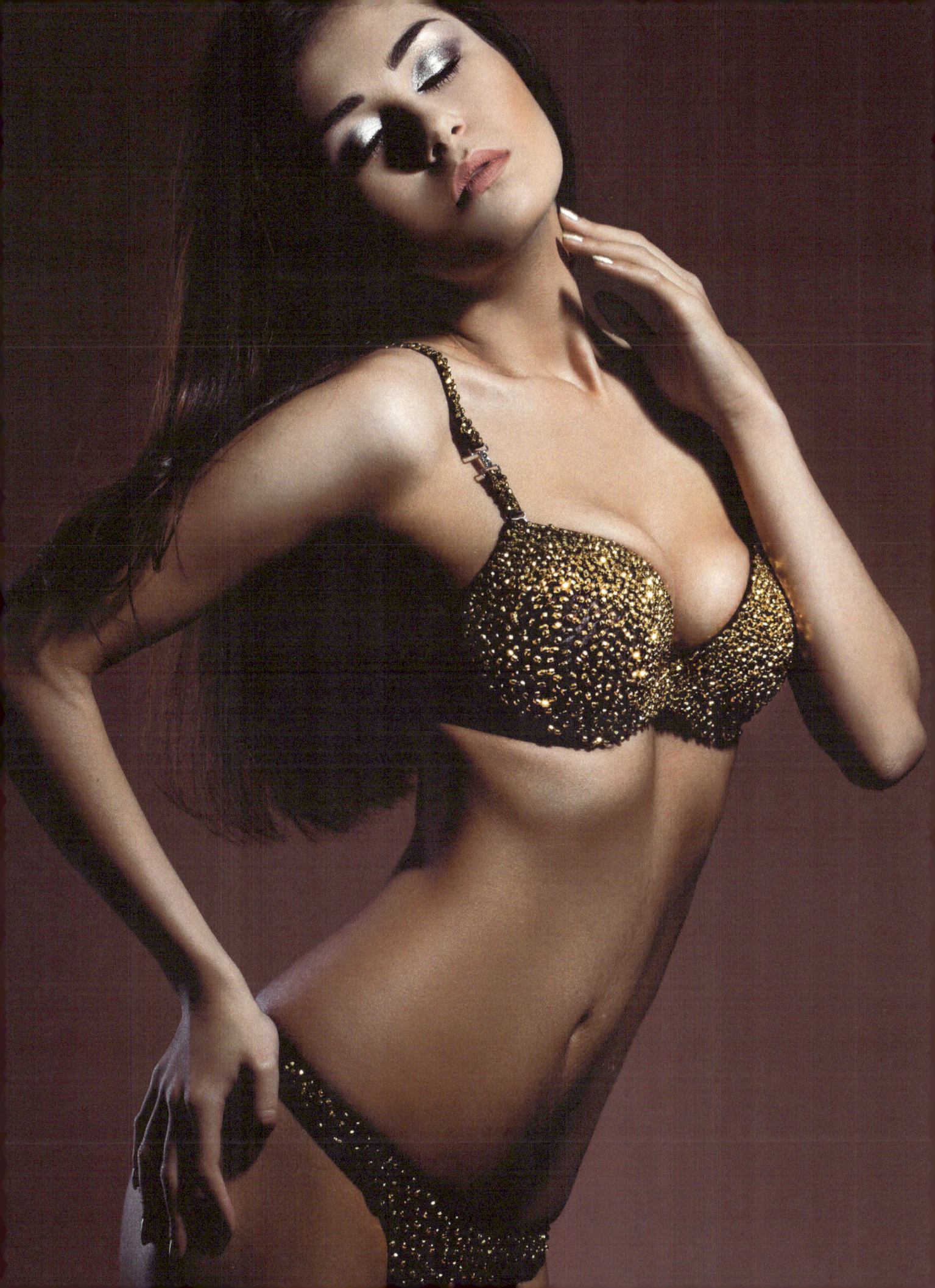

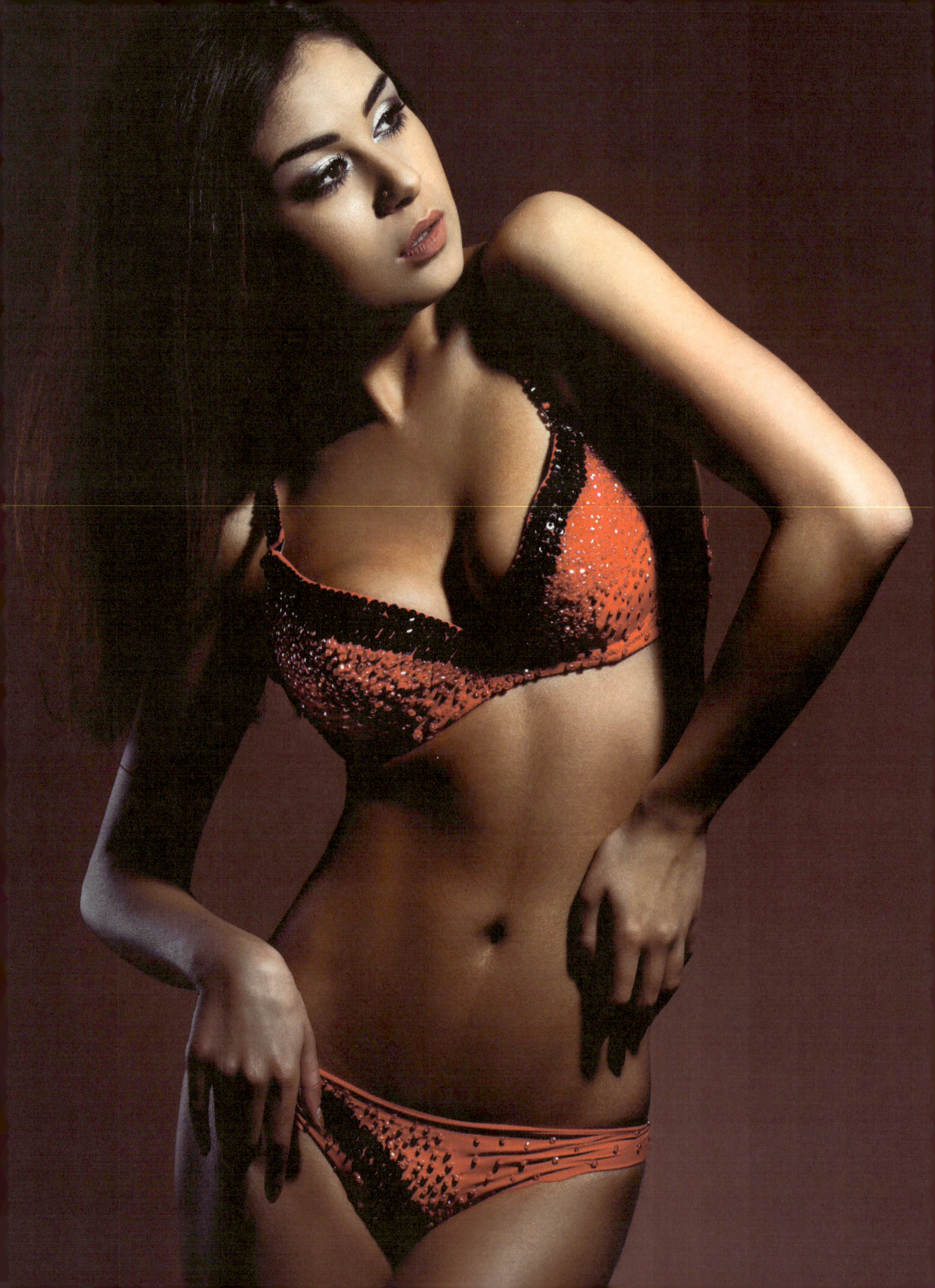

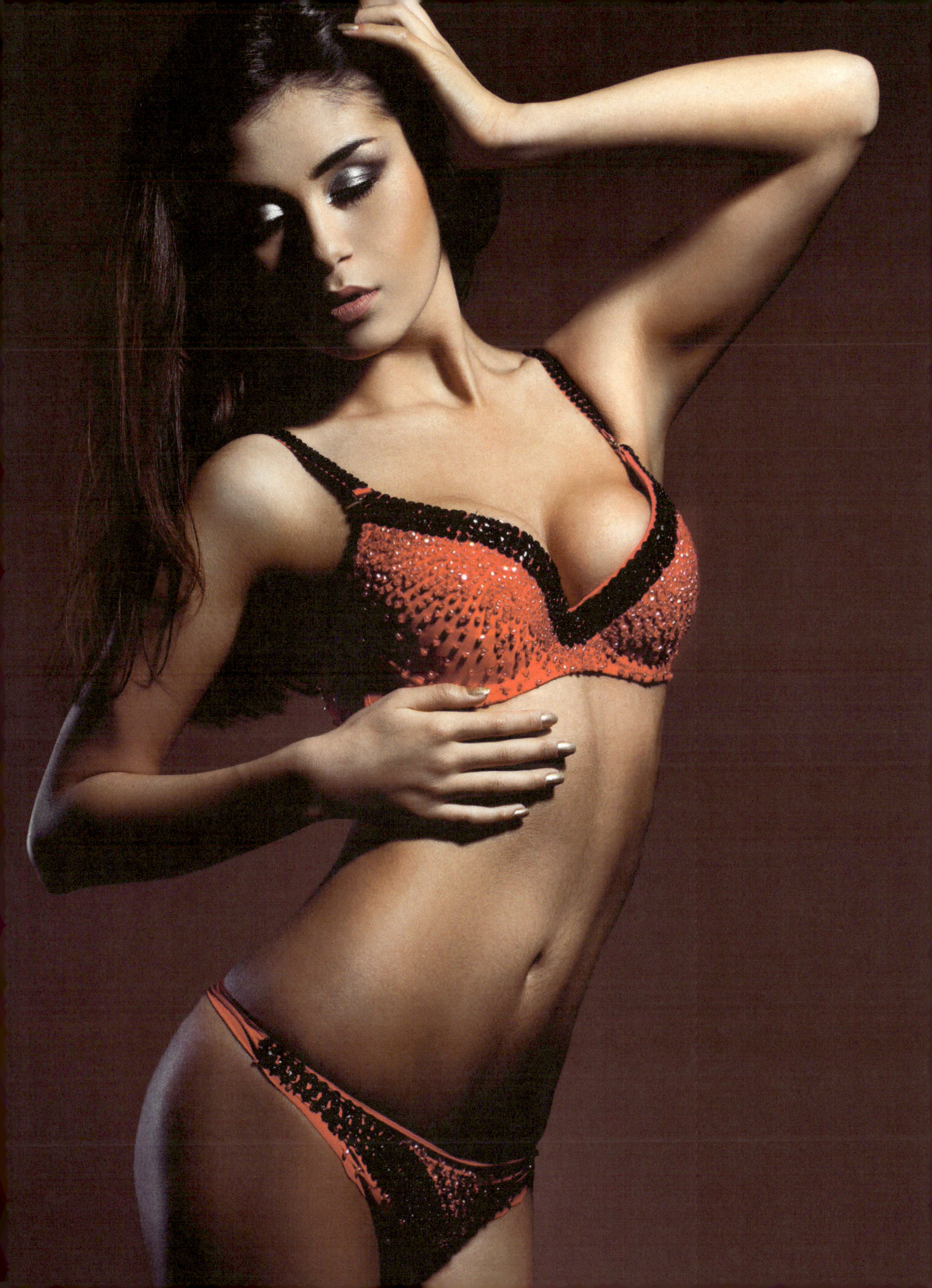

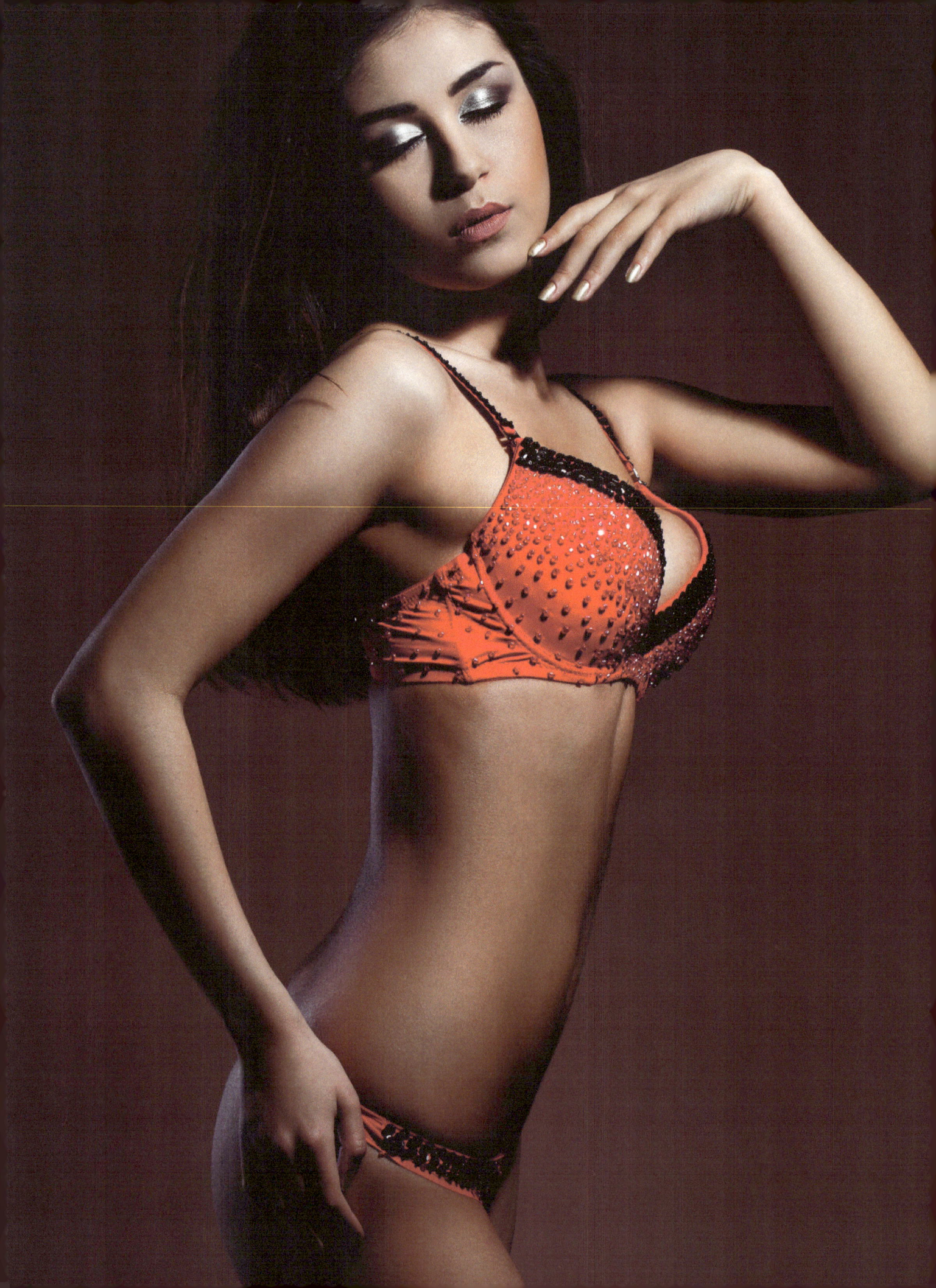

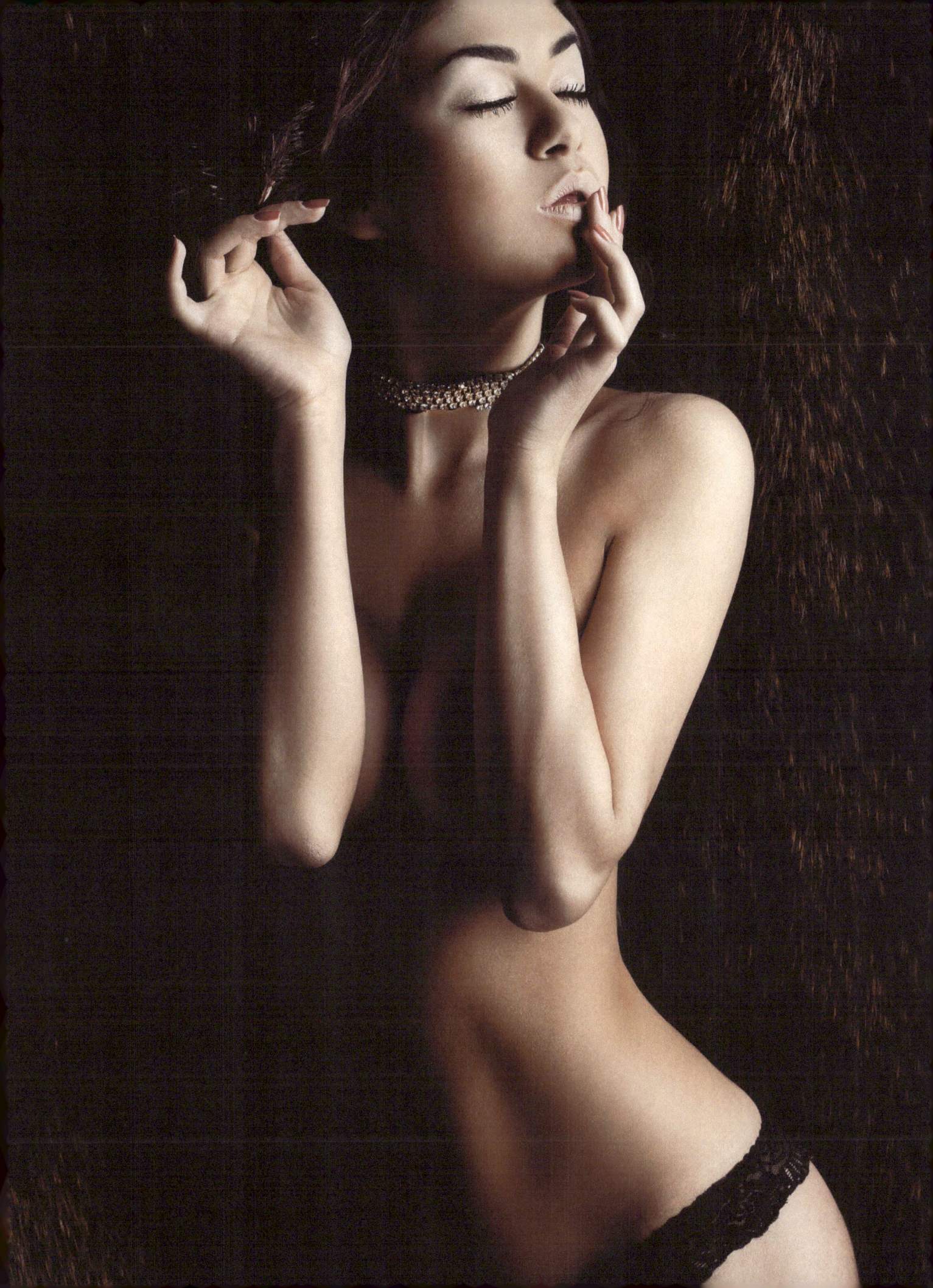

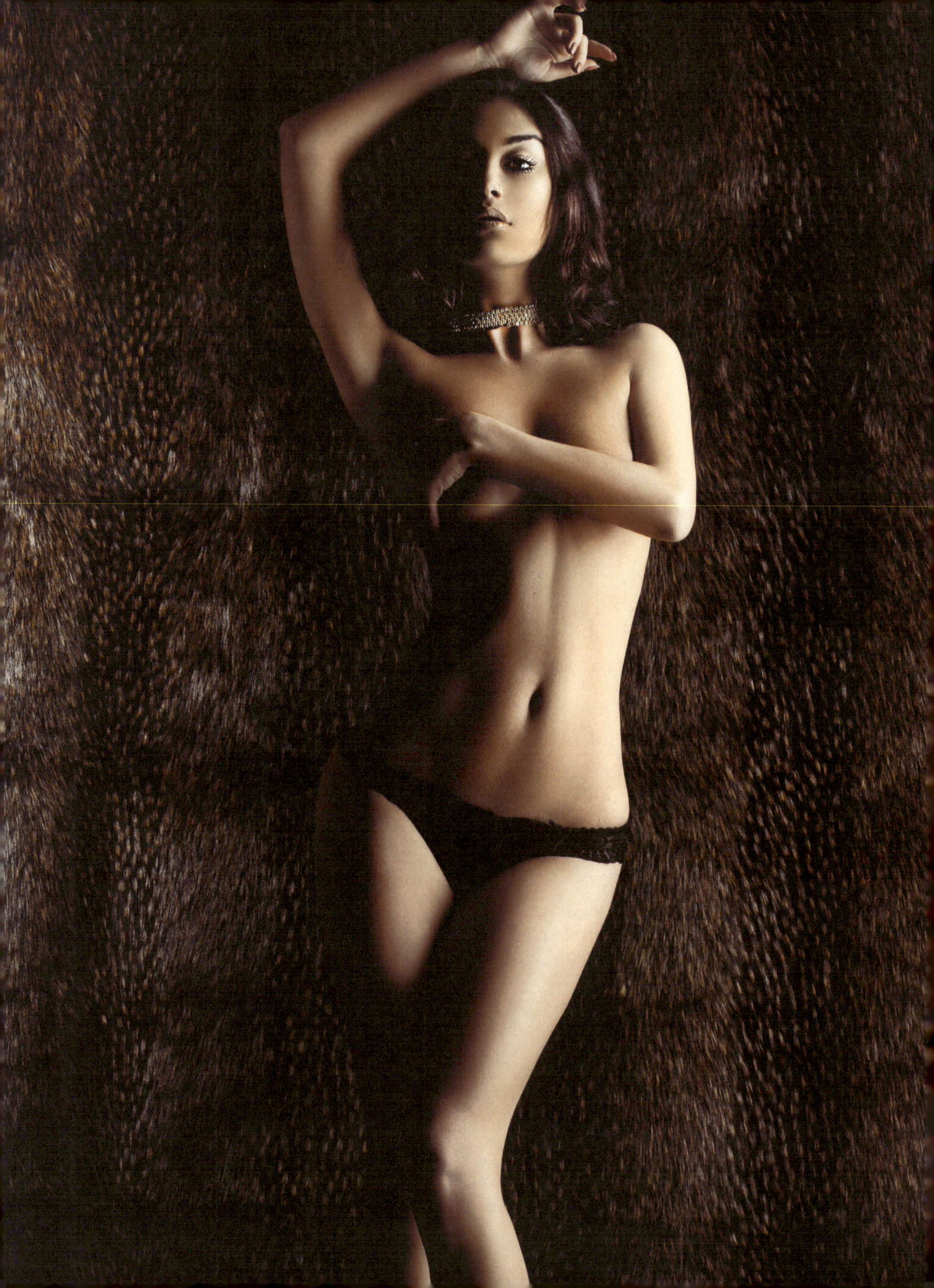

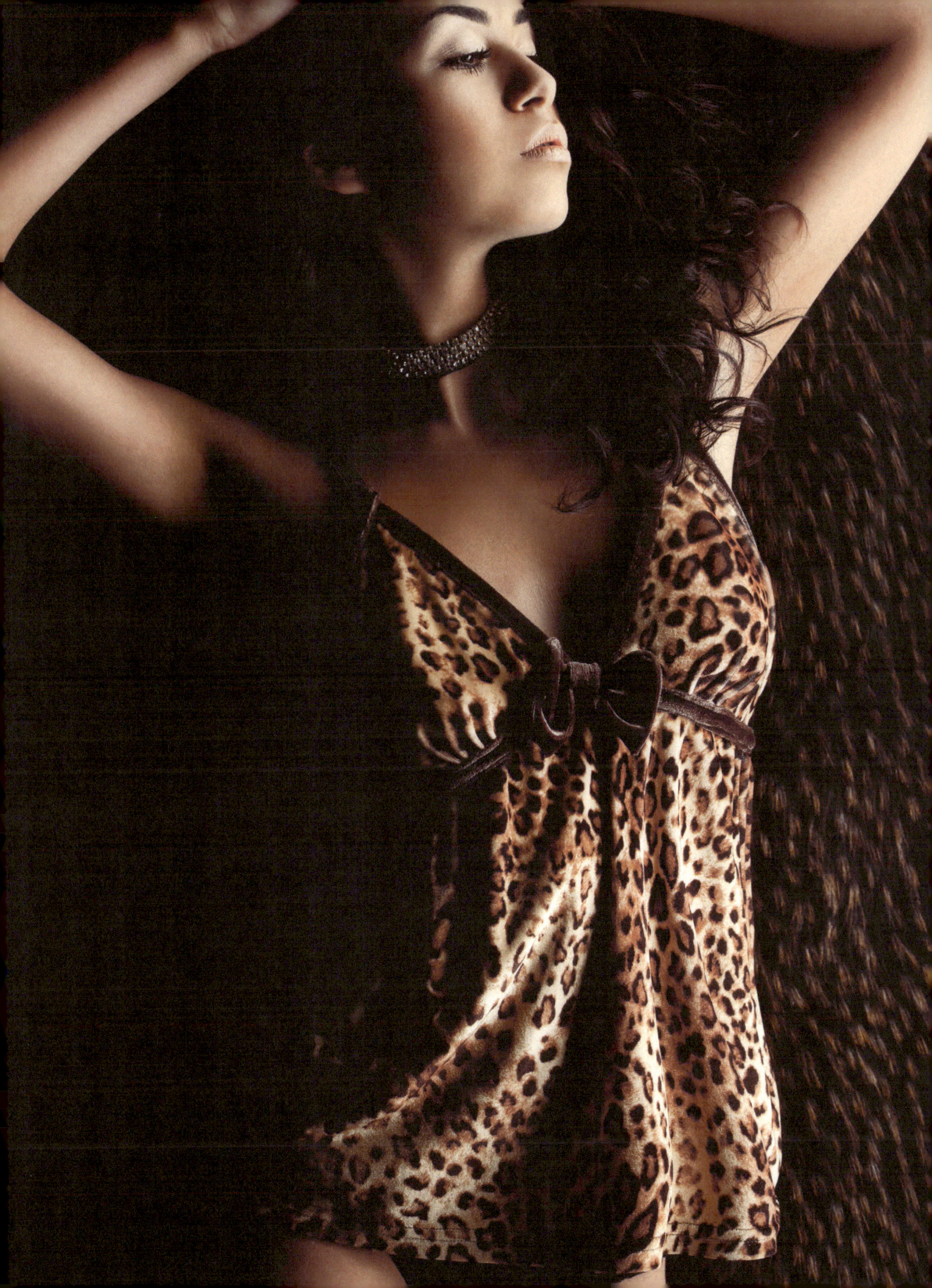

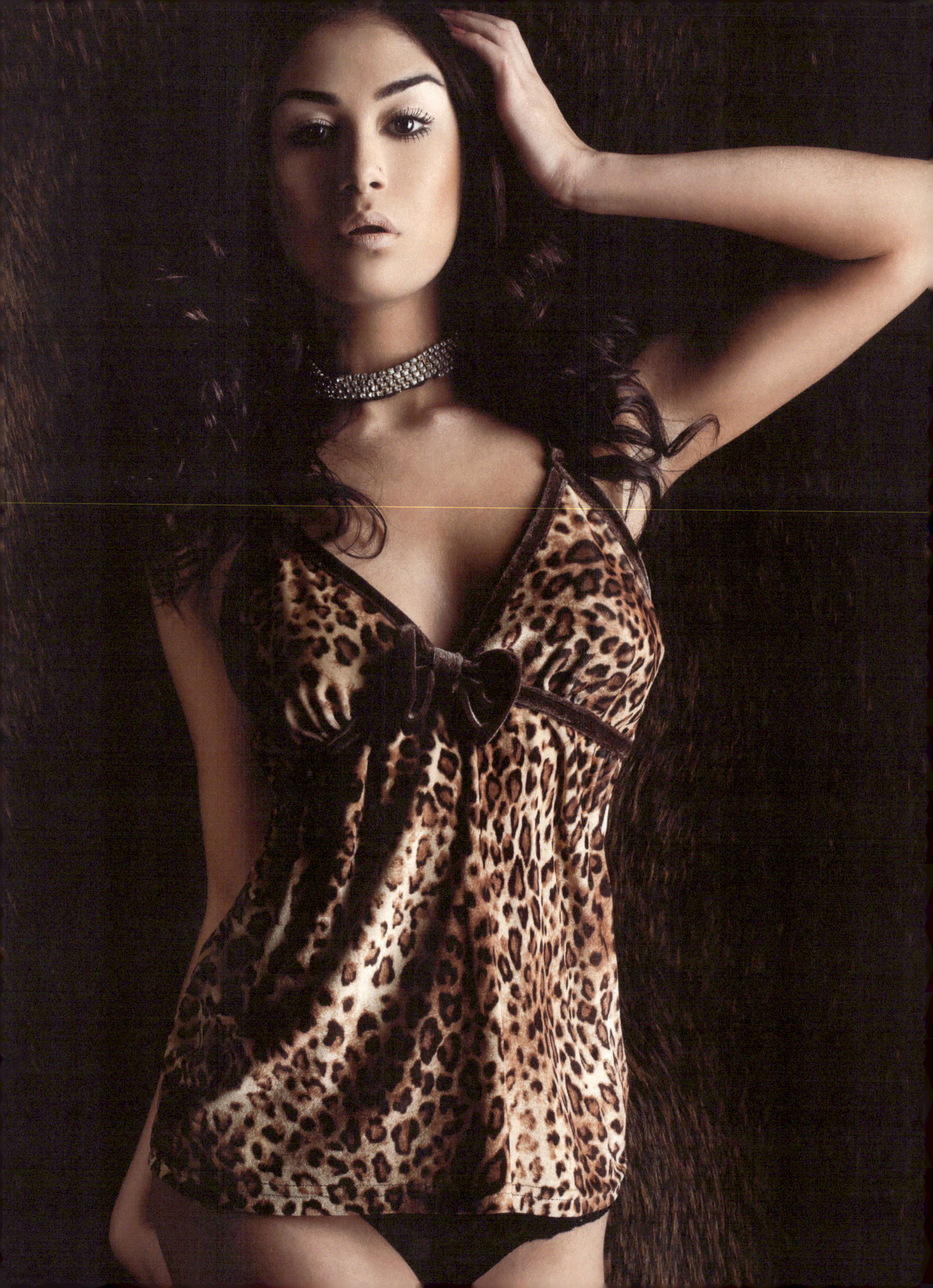

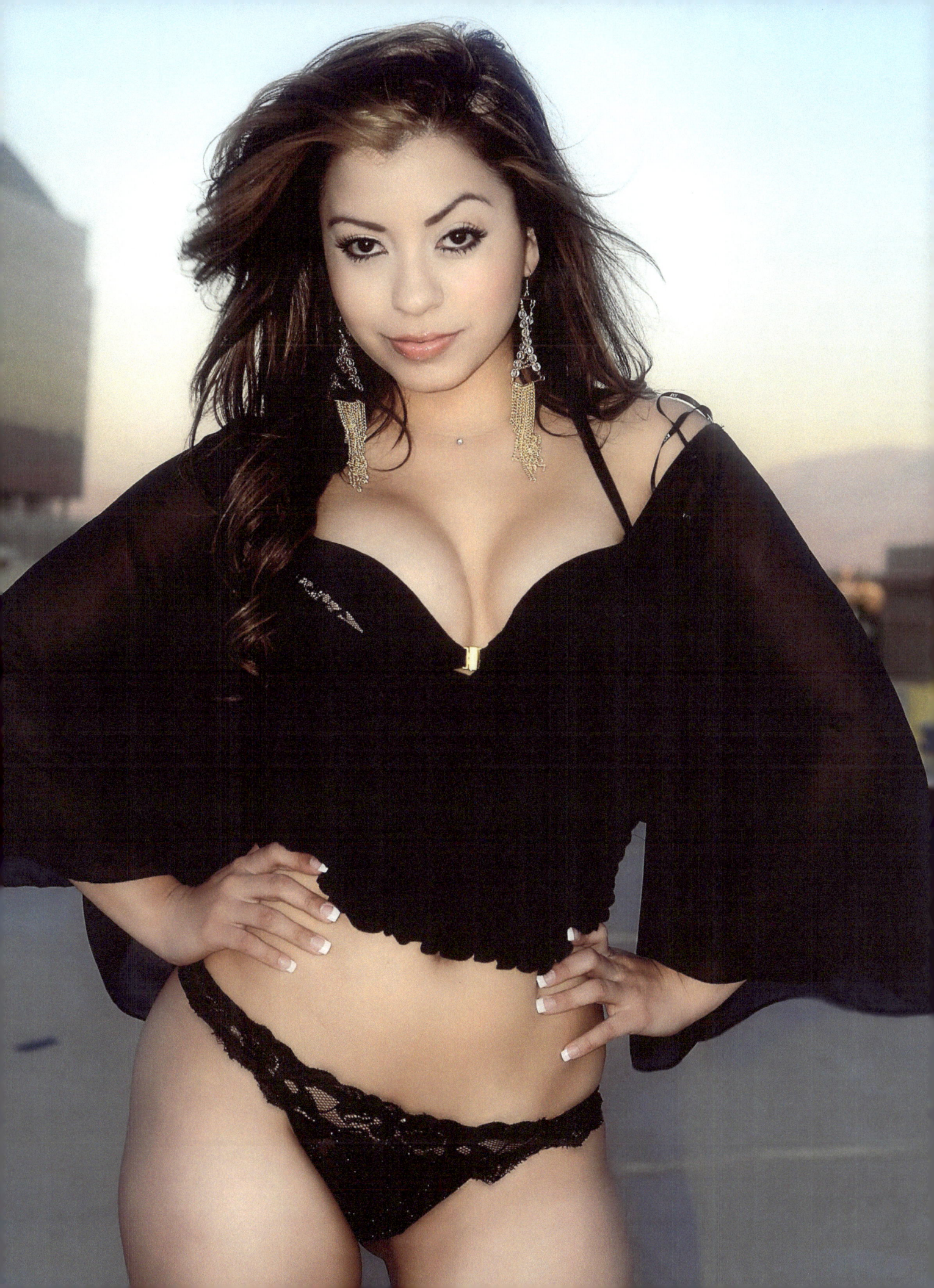

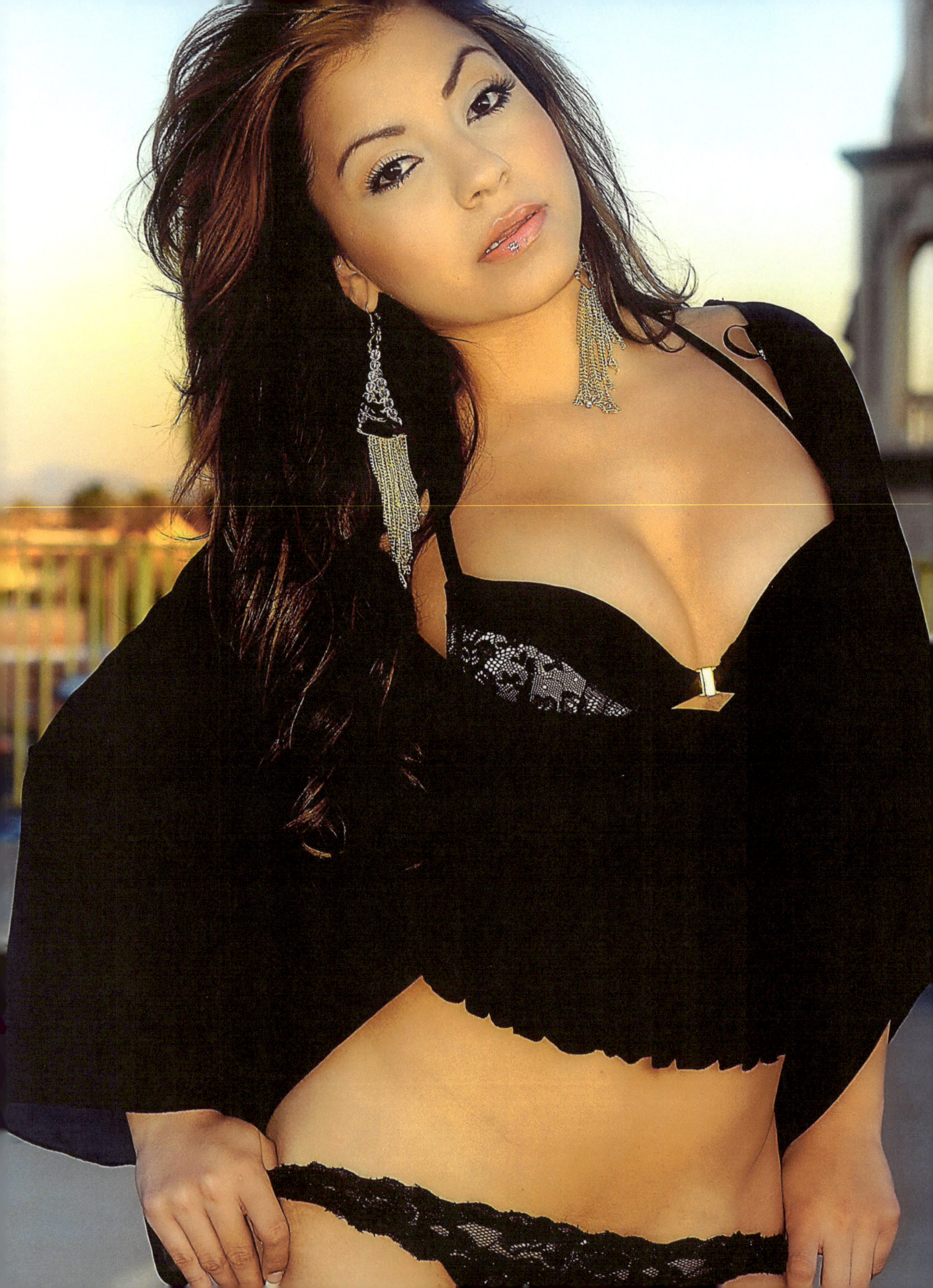

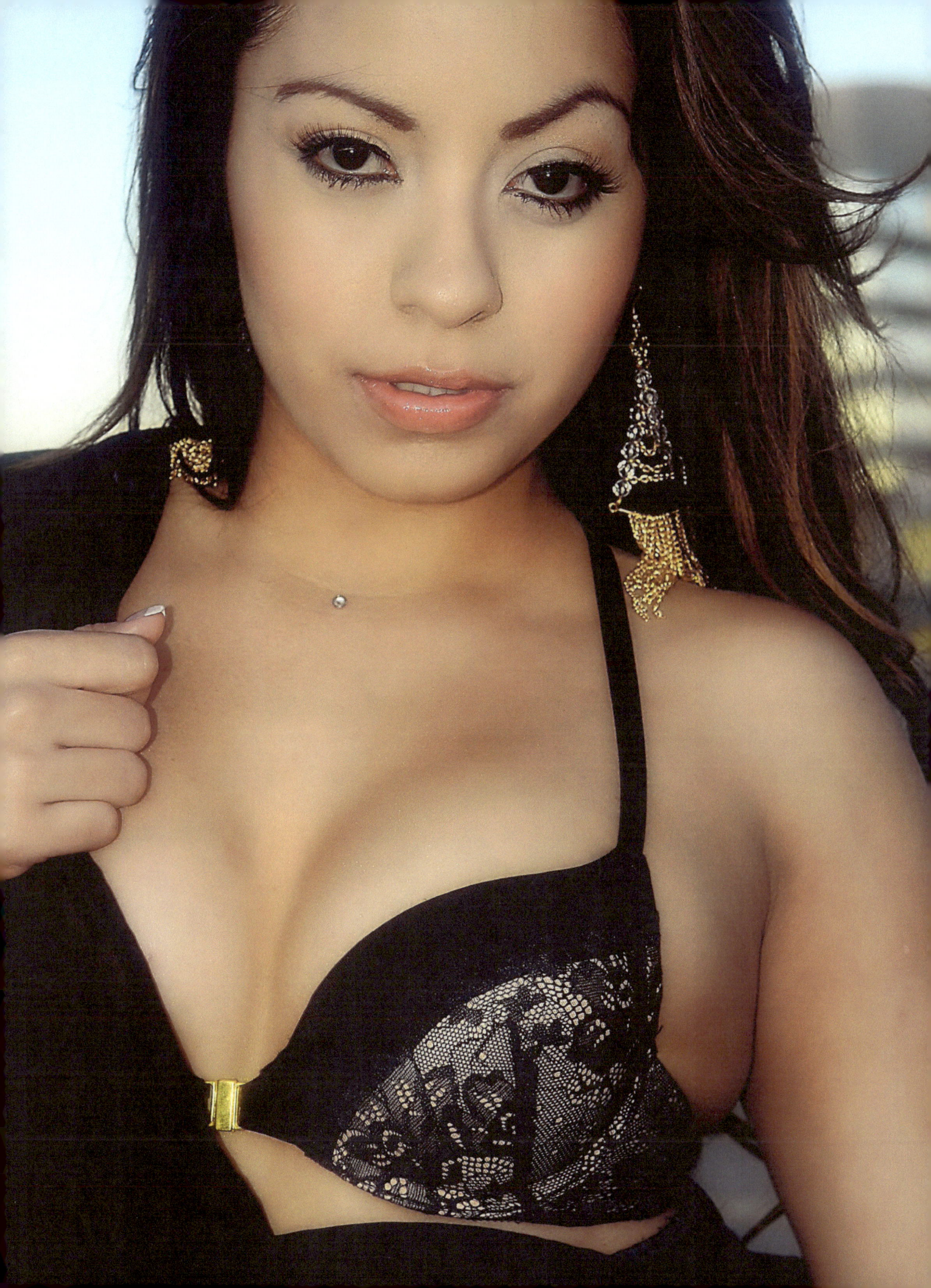

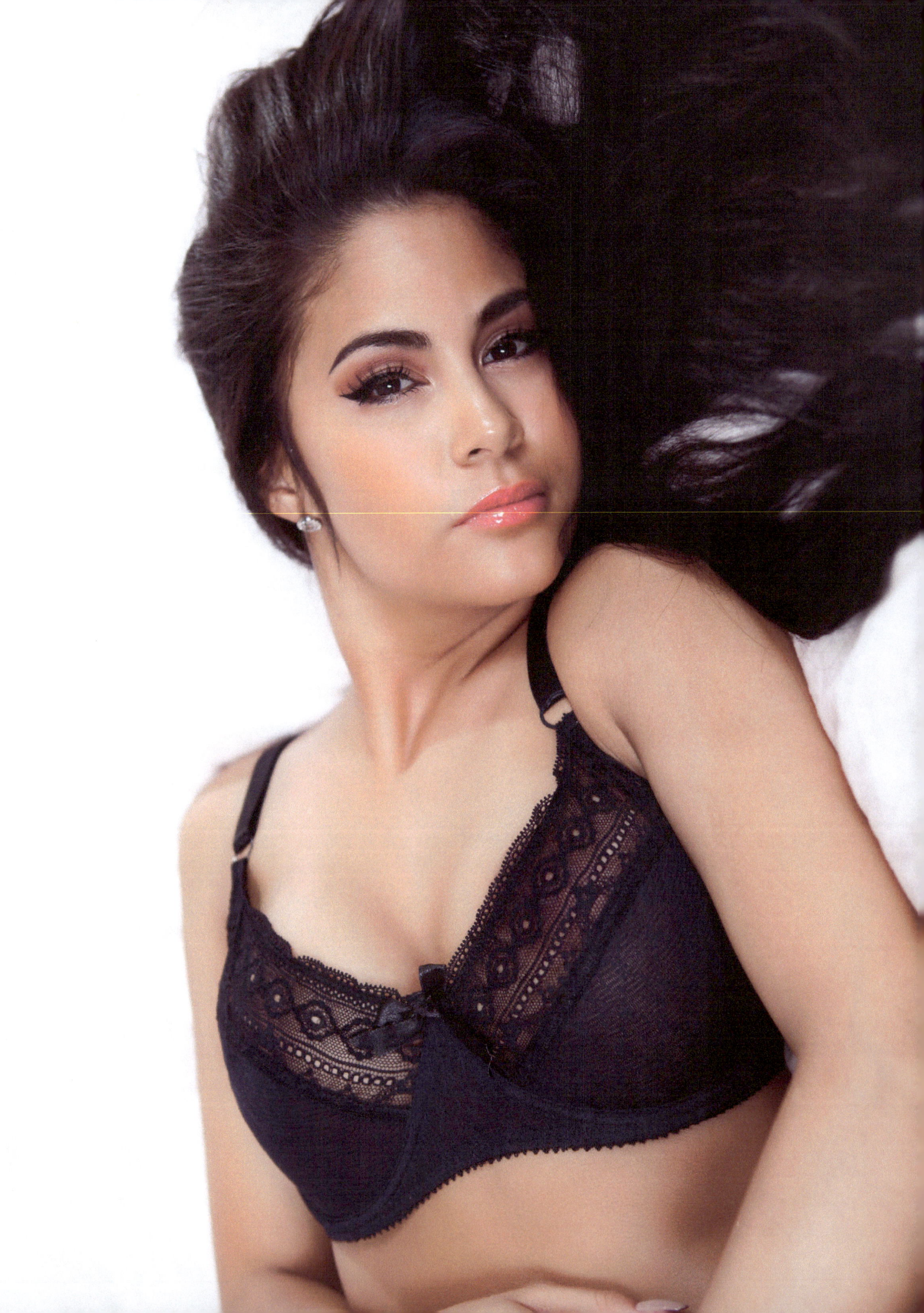

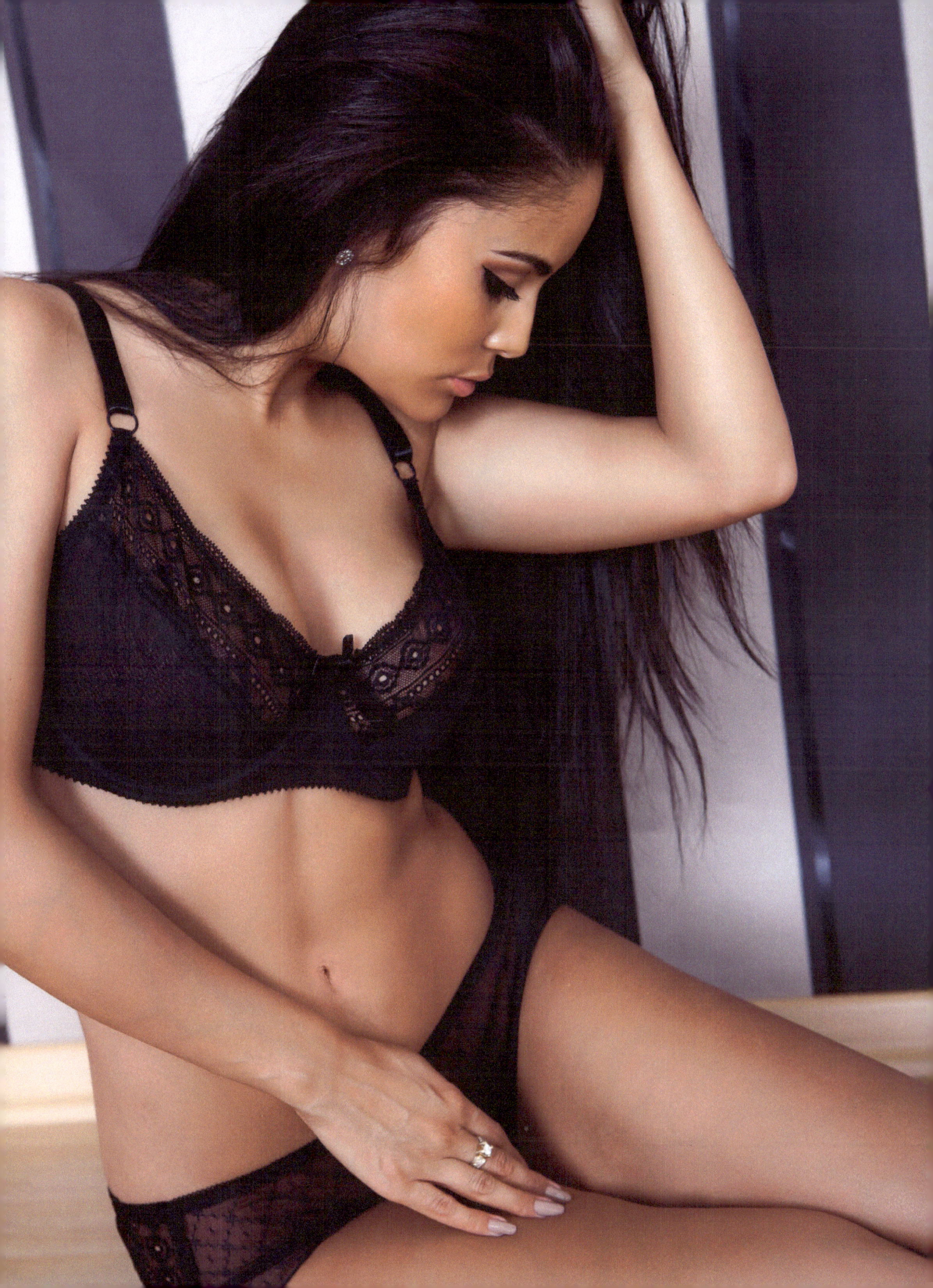

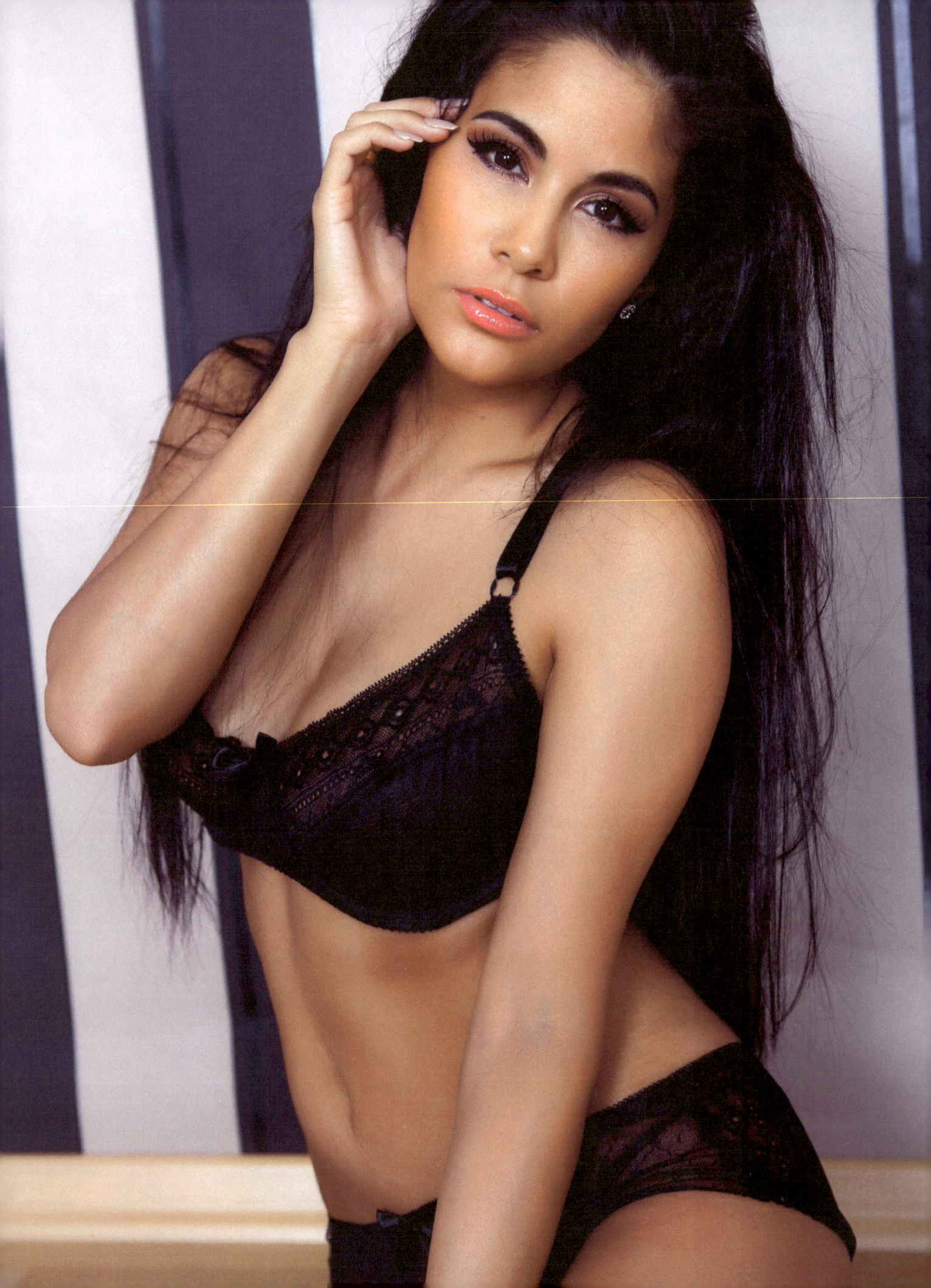

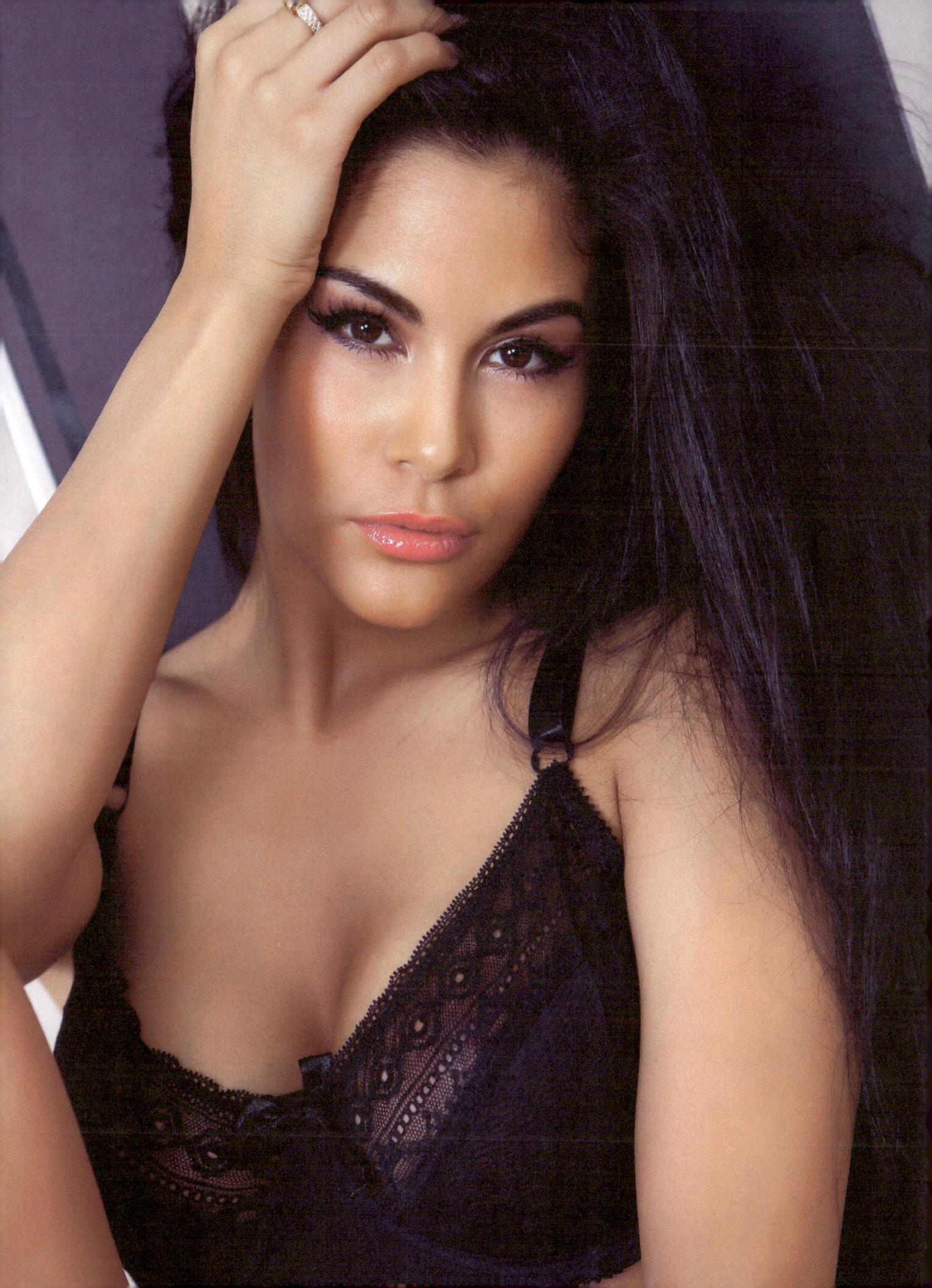

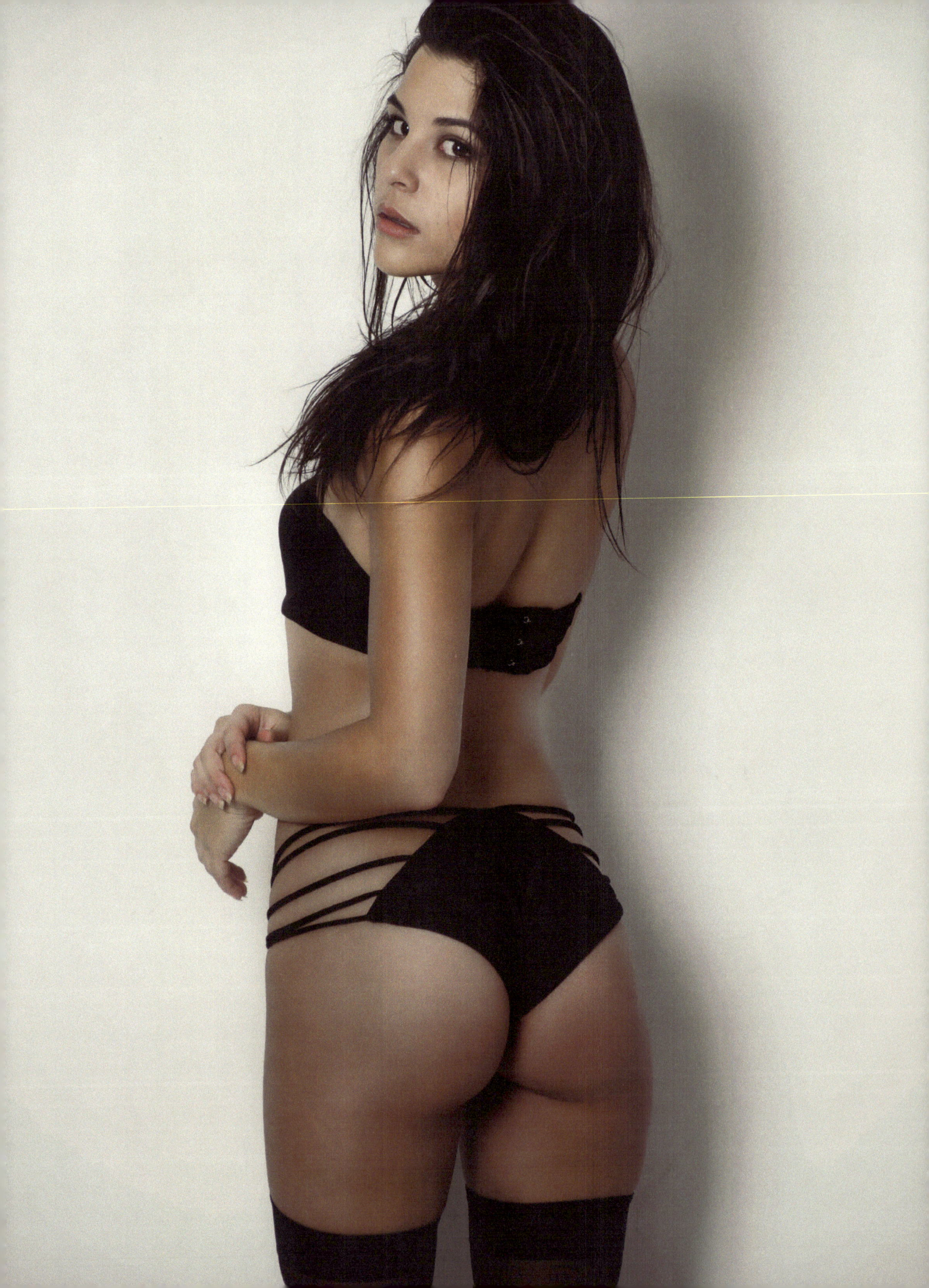

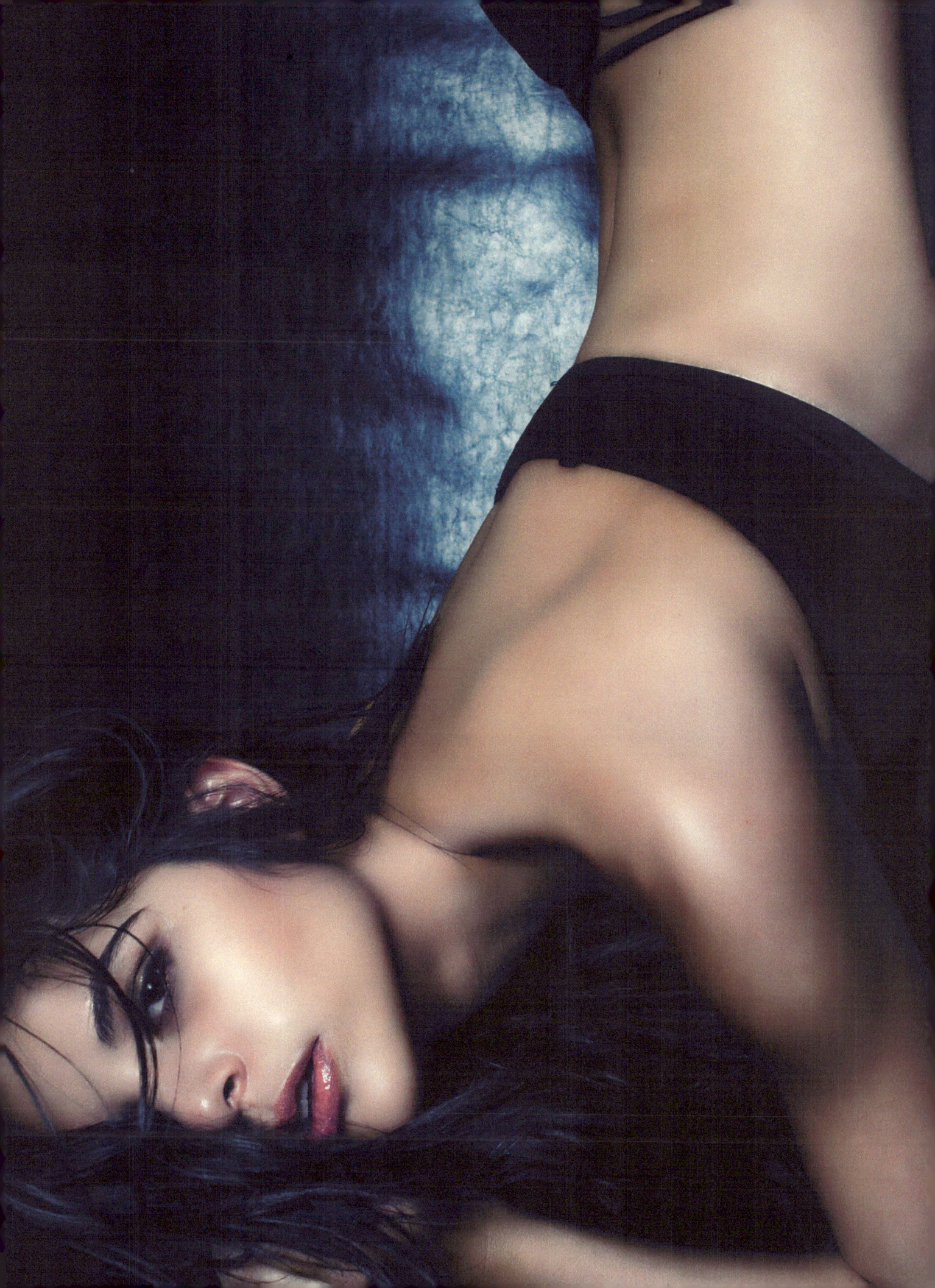

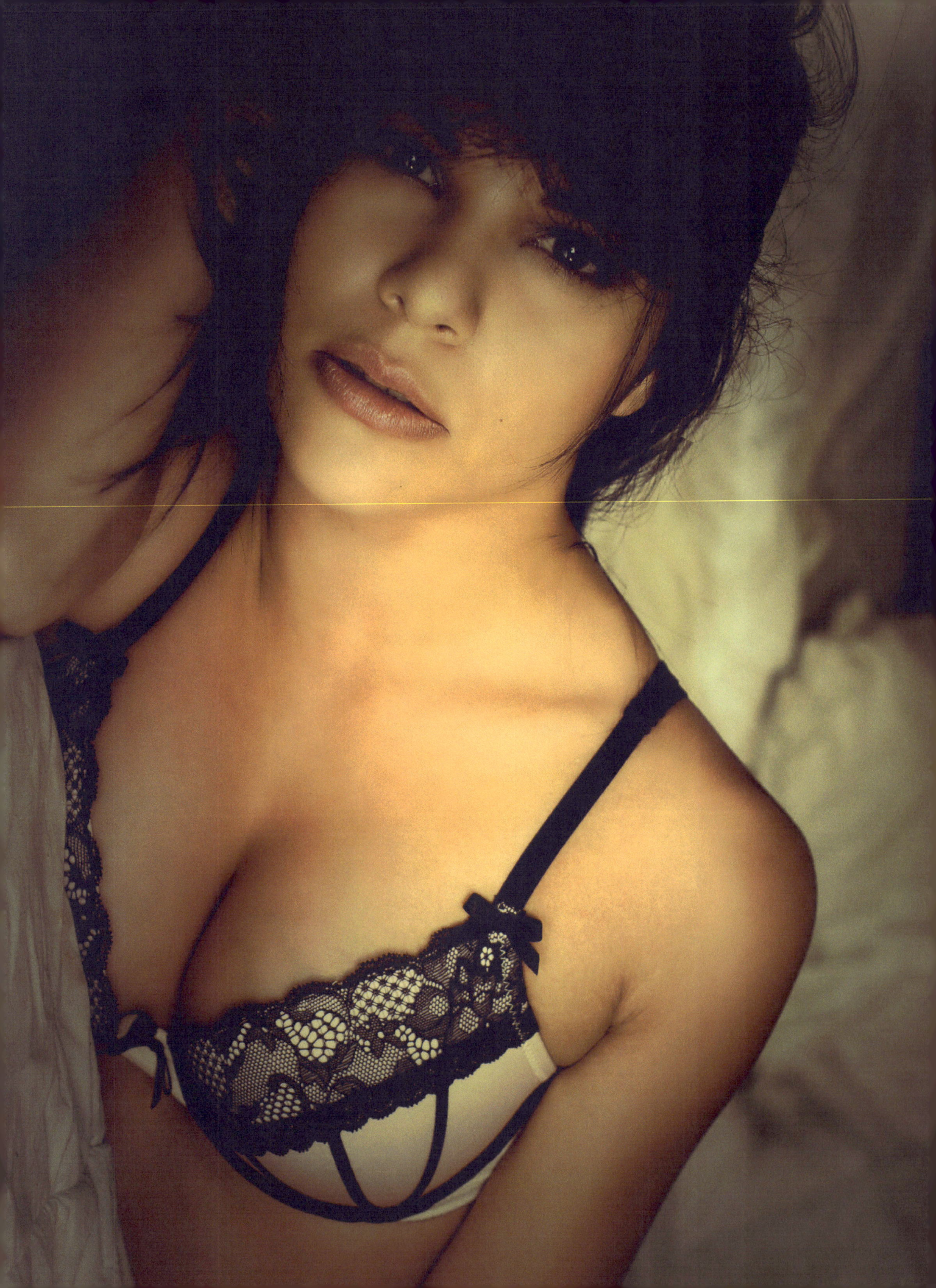

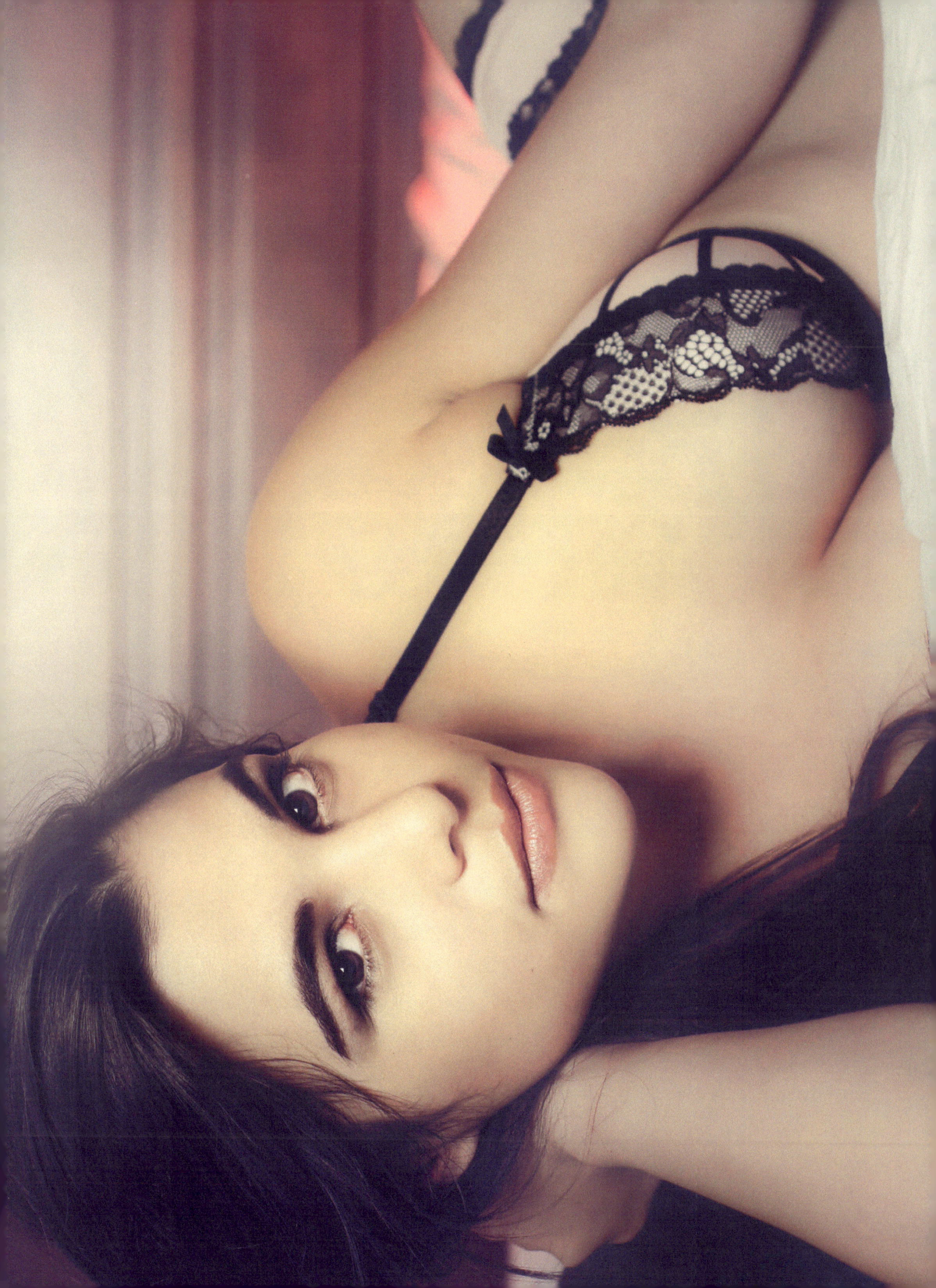

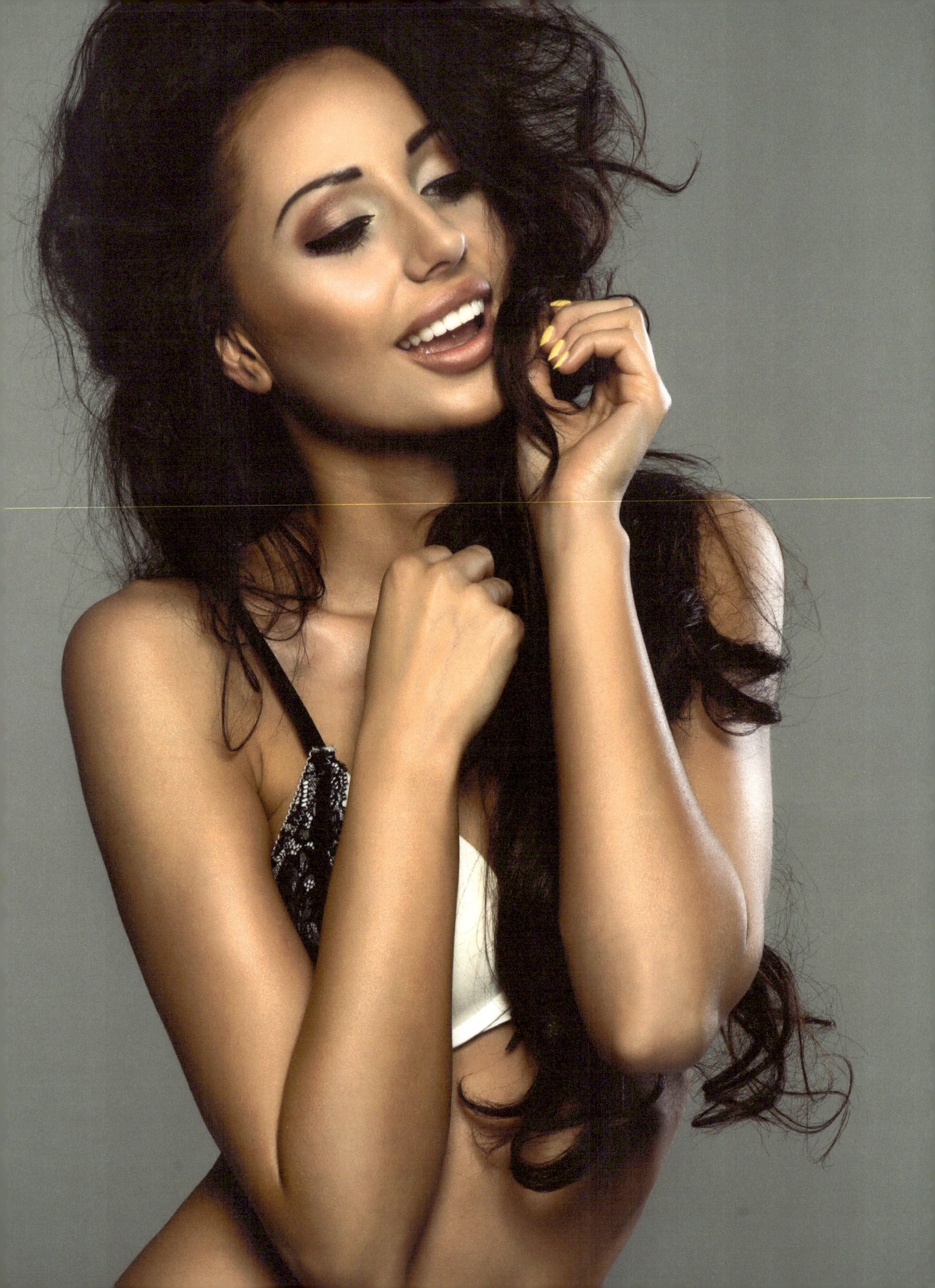

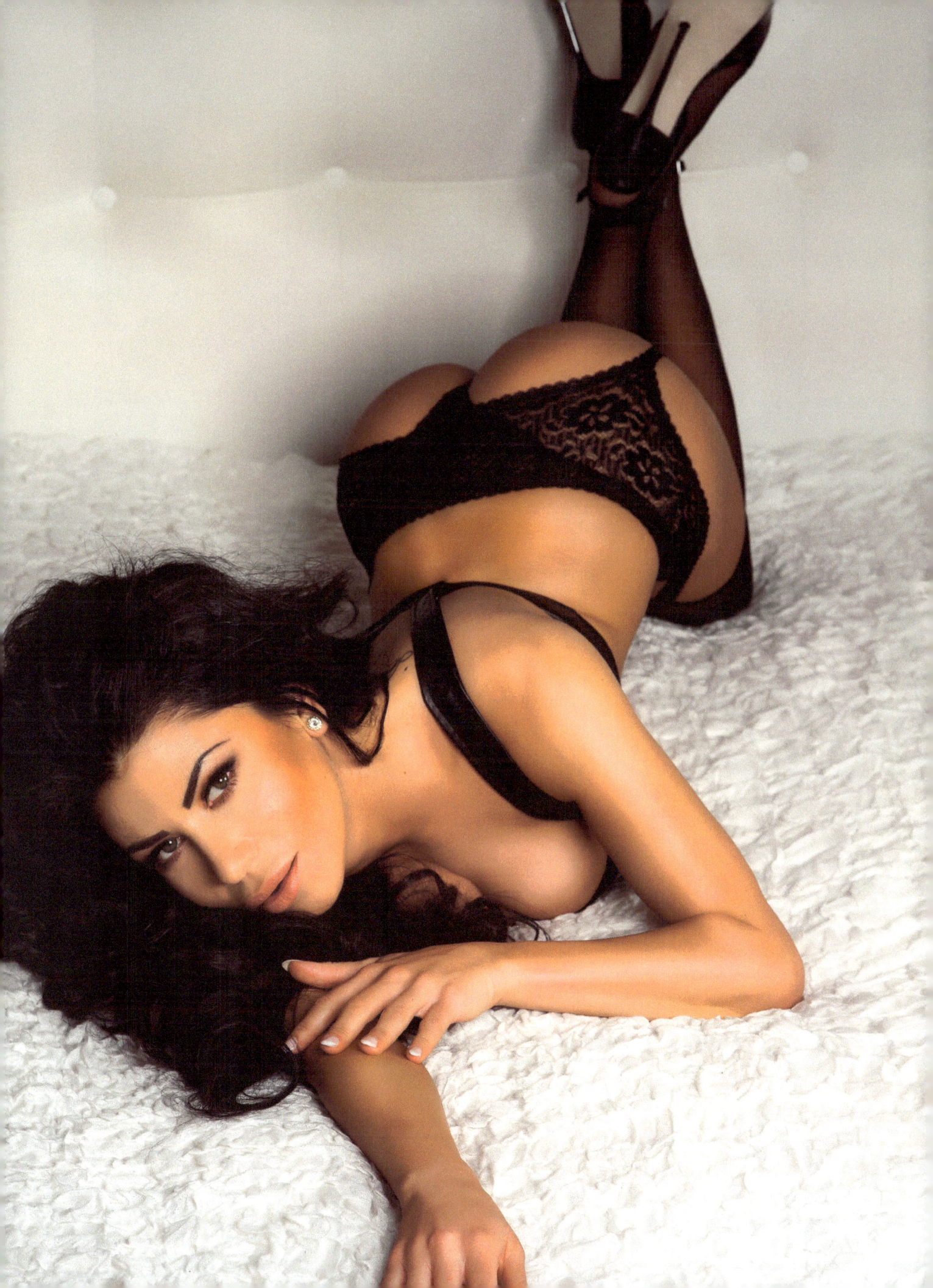

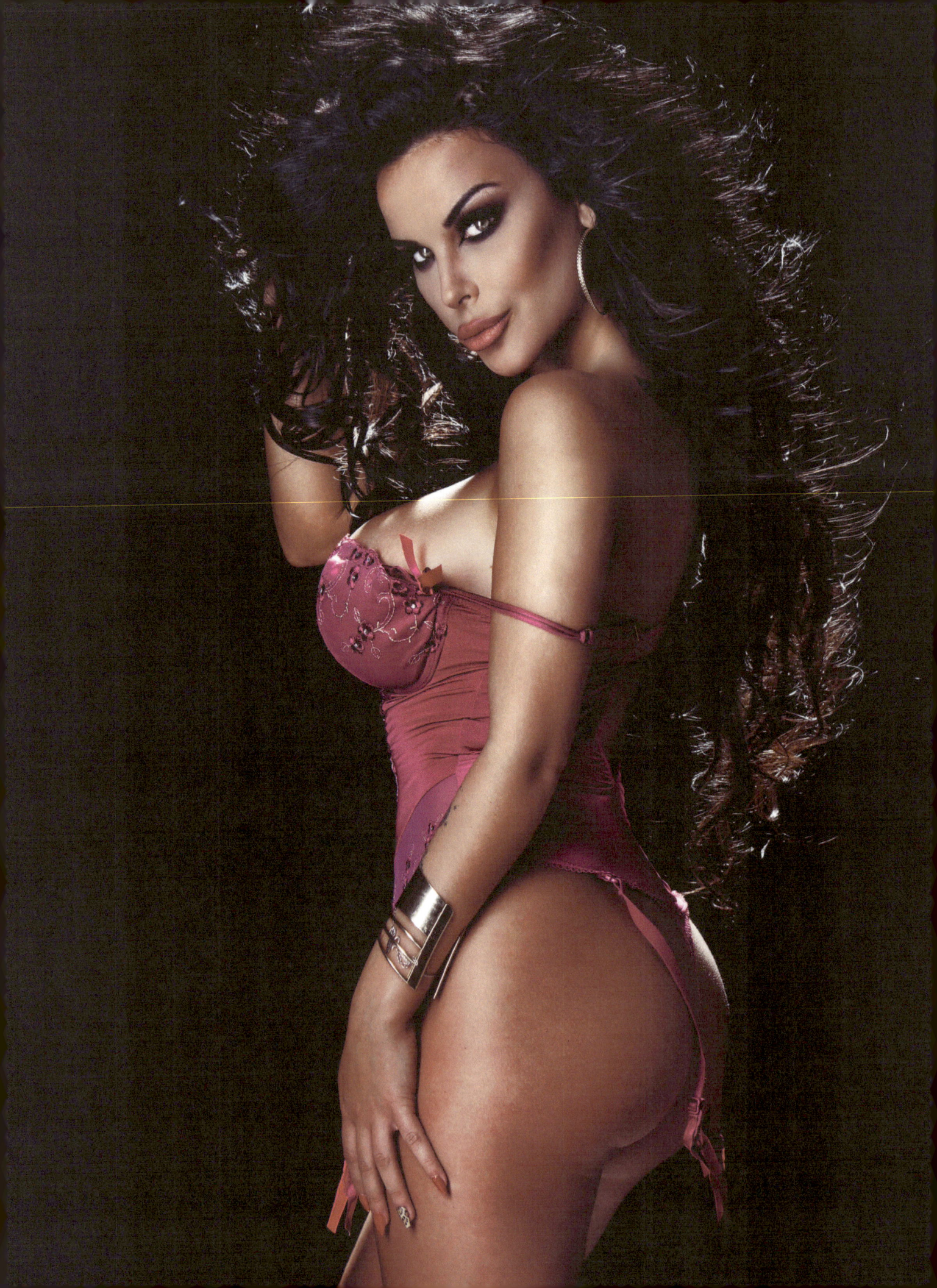

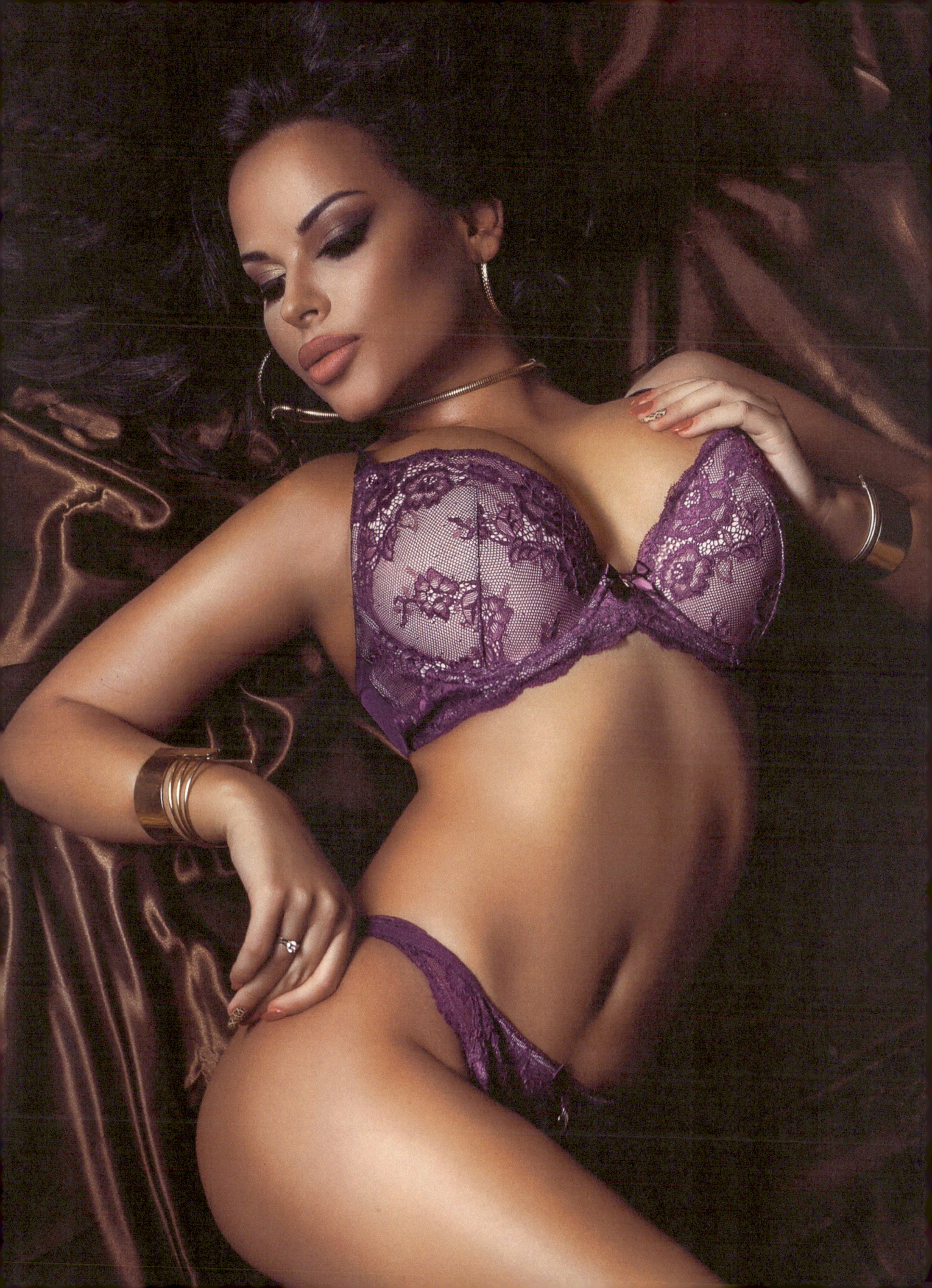

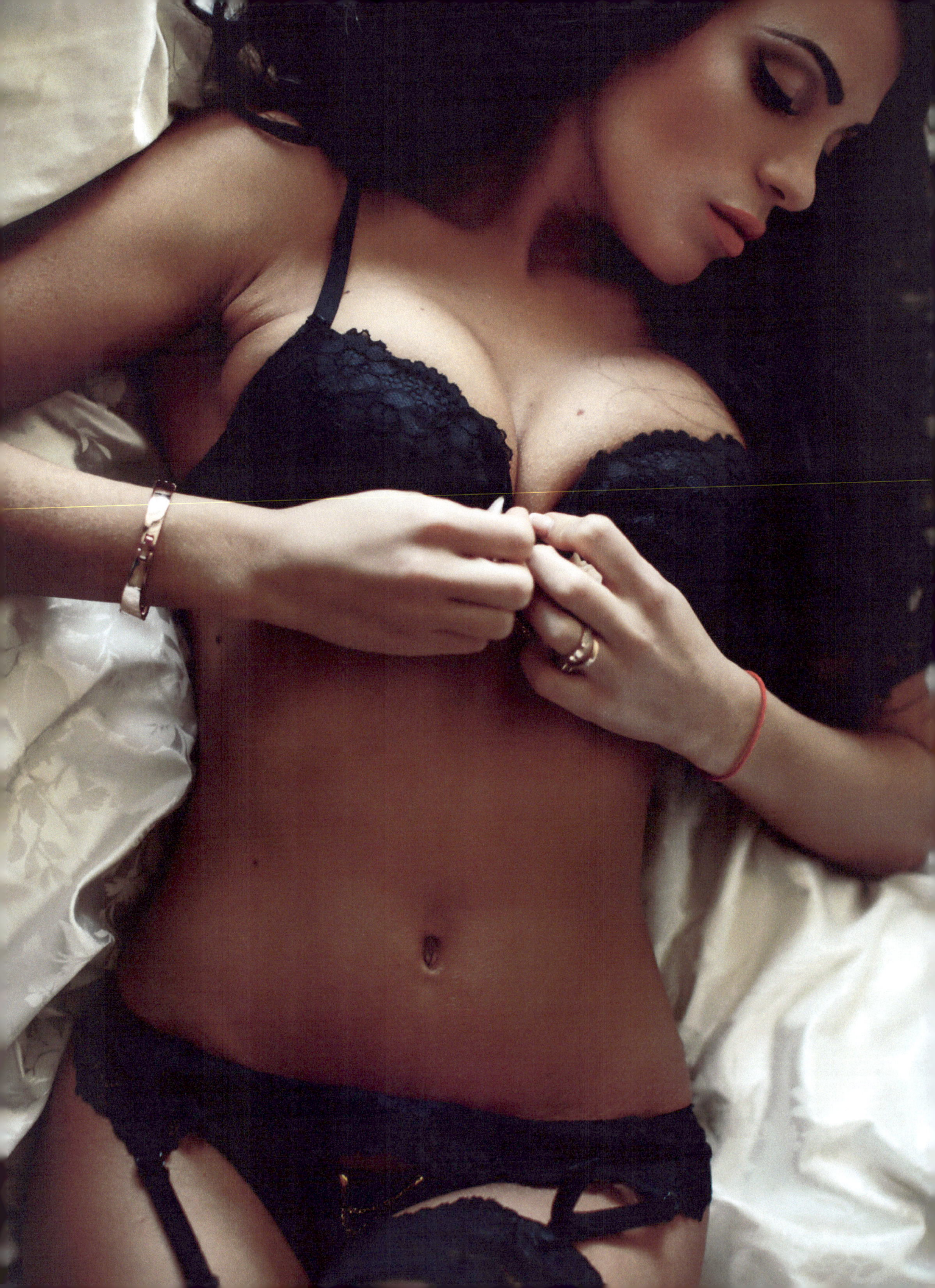

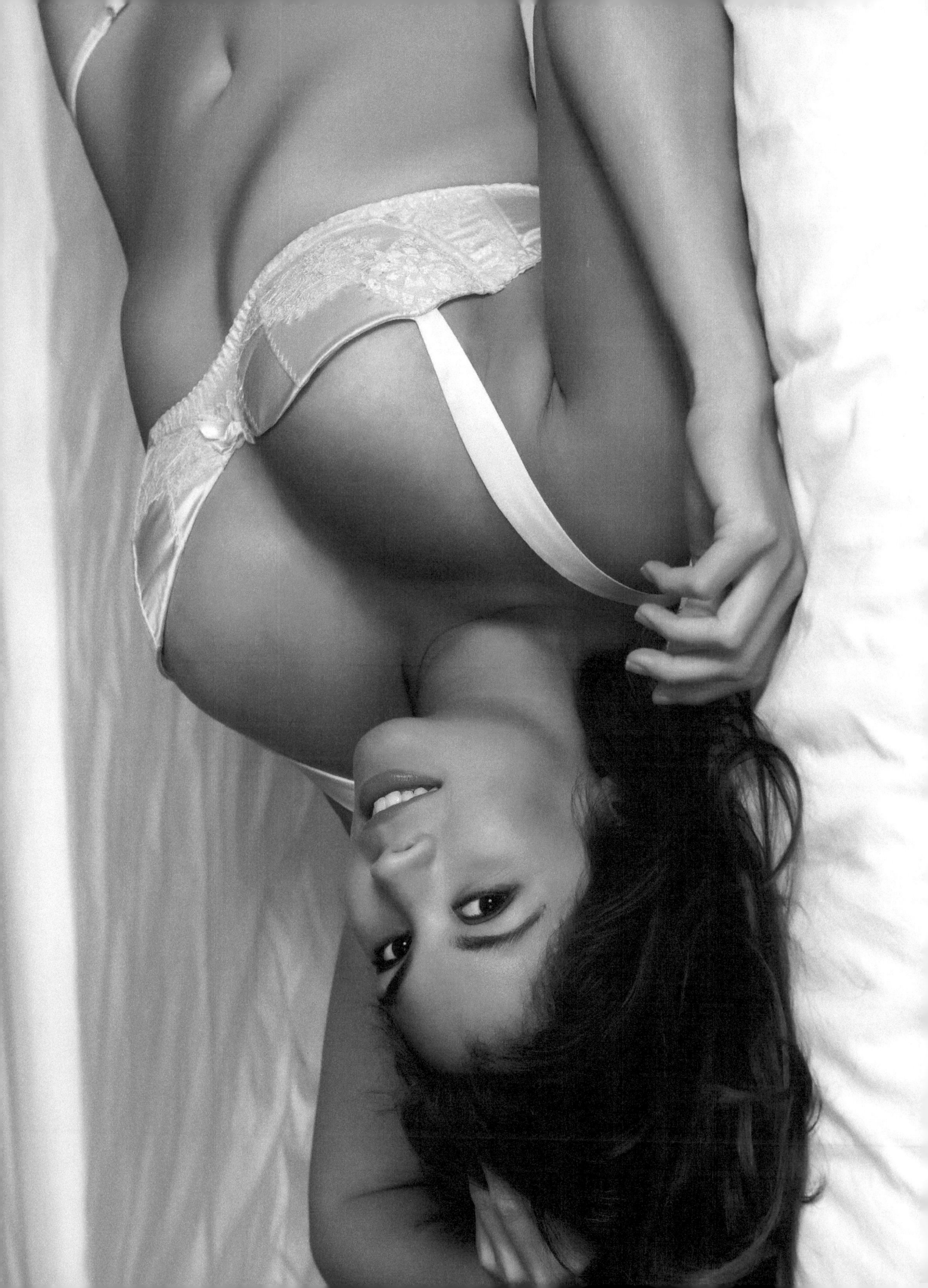

www.ingramcontent.com/pod-product-compliance
Lightning Source LLC
Chambersburg PA
CBHW041305180526
45172CB00003B/978